CHILD LABOR AND THE URBAN THIRD WORLD

Toward a New Understanding of the Problem

Subrata Sankar Bagchi

University Press of America,® Inc.
Lanham · Boulder · New York · Toronto · Plymouth, UK

Copyright © 2010 by
University Press of America,® Inc.
4501 Forbes Boulevard
Suite 200
Lanham, Maryland 20706
UPA Acquisitions Department (301) 459-3366

Estover Road
Plymouth PL6 7PY
United Kingdom

Library of Congress Control Number: 2010932649
ISBN: 978-0-7618-5298-8 (paperback : alk. paper)
eISBN: 978-0-7618-5299-5

To my mother

Table of Contents

List of Tables

PREFACE

In this book the author has tried to develop a different understanding from the Third World perspective of the phenomenon of child labor in a Third World city like Kolkata. In this pursuit, the author explored this phenomenon in the backdrop of urban marginalization which is prevalent in these Third World cities. Urban marginalization in a Third World city, as observed in this work, is primarily the result of the state's failure to provide adequate collective consumption (basic urban services to be provided by the state to the city dwellers) to an increasing proportion of the urban population and thus rendering them marginalized. This process of marginalization is further exacerbated in the SAP (Structural Adjustment Program) regime in which the Third World states are forced to withdraw subsidies from spheres of life their nationals including collective consumption in the urban areas.

This general approach has been considered fairly extensively in this book, drawing on empirical findings from three different settlements (called here as the Population I, Population II and Population III) in the city of Kolkata which were studied intensively over a period of more than ten years, and also on the findings on national as well as international comparisons. Among the settlements studied here Population I and Population II were the squatter settlements, where the inhabitants lived without any security of tenure as well as with almost no (state mediated) urban basic services in the form of collective consumption. During this fieldwork, both these settlements were eroded from the landscape of the city of Kolkata and the acts of evicting these people were done to undertake some development projects in the city of Kolkata. Population III, on the other hand, was a recognized slum settlement where the inhabitants lived with some kind of security of tenure by virtue of an act [Calcutta *Thika* and Other Tenancies and Lands (Acquisition and Regulation) Act, 1981]. The author considered Population I and Population II as the Control Group and Population III as the Program Group. Empirical findings (mostly in quantitative term) as well as thick descriptions on the Control Group and the Program Group differ substantially in the present work. Thus we find that the people in the Program Group were in much better condition than their counterparts in the Control Group primarily due to the security of tenure they had obtained through the legislation. Security of tenure in fact had initiated the process towards a betterment in life in the Program Group of population and then the people in the Program Group with the advent of time further moved that process with their own endeavors as well as with the help of some development program taken up for them.

In the first chapter of this book the author tried to introduce the work and discussed on the background of the work with particular reference to the works on Indian urban scenario. This chapter raised the issues under the present topic and presented the background to the issues, including previous studies touching the similar issues. The second chapter critically reviewed the existing definitions and concepts on child labor which was imperative to look beyond the present body of knowledge on this issue. The third chapter actually builds the central argument in favor of a new understanding of child labor in the urban Third World. In this chapter, along with the summarizing the view of the definitions and concepts on child labor, the author briefly described the magnitude of the problem of child labor and the national and international initiatives to ameliorate and/or eradicate the problem of child labor. Then the chapter actually entered into the argument with a brief account of the research design followed by the description findings of author's decade-long fieldwork where he took up various aspects of the population like the profile of the populations, educational aspects of the population, integration with the urban life, economic aspects of the population, population and educational profiles of the child laborers and the economic profile of the child laborers. The last chapter stressed on the need for a paradigm shift in the present body of analyses on child labor particularly in the urban Third World.

For commenting on part of this manuscript the author is most grateful to Arnab Das and Siddhartha DasGupta. The author also wishes to thank Dipak Shome for printing part of this manuscript. He is also immensely grateful to Dr. Nibedita Chakrabarti, Geeta Bagchi, Urmi Bagchi, Priyadarsini Sengupta, Soma RayChaudhuri and Subrata Basak for their invaluable contributions at the various stages of this work.

Subrata Sankar Bagchi
Kolkata, West Bengal
India

CHAPTER 1

INTRODUCING THE WORK

This work started during the early years of 1990s when India as a nation started entering into the GATT/WTO regime through its economic reform policies implemented from 1991, immediately after a balance of payment crisis with the proposition of enhanced growth, efficiency and the prosperity of people. But from the experiences of other nations, particularly in the Latin American and African countries where the GATT/WTO regime was in practice from 1980s, it was apprehended by several experts that behind the promises of "good life" for all through these policies there existed the grim realities of increased inequality, deprivation, threat to livelihood, disintegration of social order, displacement and landlessness, alienation and violence as well as a growing fear of the future. A huge number of people in the cities as well as in the rural areas of these countries have already been marginalized due to SAP (Structural Adjustment Program) when the Indian government adopted the SAP regime in the early 1990s. Therefore, it was quite natural to apprehend that a decimation of similar kind of, if not a more aggravated form, would happen in India after a few years under SAP regime. This apprehension was validated by the later developments in India.

The author's decision to study urban marginalization and child labor in a Third World city like Kolkata during those initial year under the SAP regime was prompted by the realization that this issue poised to become one the one of the biggest challenge to the collective survival of the majority of people in the Third World. The phenomenon of urban marginalization has been conceived here as the inability of market economy or state policies to provide adequate shelter and urban basic services (explained here as collective consumption) to an increasing proportion of urban population. Urban marginalization is viewed here as the result of a struggle over urban space among the different sections of population. The author explored how this struggle has been exacerbated by different SAP-induced measures, which include withdrawal of state subsidies in different key sectors like education, health, basic services like water supply, sanitation, sewage etc. undertaken by the local and the national government. Another factor, as evident from this work, that accelerated this process of urban marginalization was the pressure on the authorities to undertake different city development or city beautification projects even at the cost of displacing so-called illegal settlements as the cities were showcased in an effort to attract global capital in the state. Thus one can observe in the Third World cities like Kolkata that a huge proportion of population does not have any security of tenure of the land on which they live and their settlements are, therefore, frequently subjected to forced evictions by the civic authorities citing various reasons like road building, city beautification, implementing development projects etc. These evictions, as observed in this study, often caused a fraying of key relationships essential for a survival network of protection to these people and frequently resulted in a further deterioration of living condition from a level that was already well below that considered adequate (Bagchi 2004, 2005).

This research, which spanned over a decade, was based on intensive anthropological fieldwork in the city of Kolkata among the marginalized people. The author observed that the poverty as well as marginalization of population in a Third World city had become integral part in the present model of neo-liberal development as it had not only widened social and economic disparities but forced new groups of people into poverty and dislocated many marginalized people from their existing support systems. This study showed how a huge proportion of marginalized population in a Third World city like Kolkata had become marginalized both in terms of urban space, as they did not have any security of tenure of the land on which they lived, and in various essential aspects of their livelihoods. Their living conditions had already worsened during this SAP regime as the local or other authorities could not provide the basic services of these people who could not afford to buy those services. This study revealed that these marginalized people in a Third World city like Kolkata not only joined in huge numbers in the informal sector as low-paid, less-profitable irregular worker; these people released their children to a ruthless labor market at a very tender age. The problem of child labor is viewed in this work as a survival strategy of the marginalized people which compelled the parents to release their children (under 14 years of age) for underpaid work in the informal sector (or very rarely in the formal sector) of economy in conditions that were harmful or potentially harmful to the child.

This study was focused on three different settlements in the city of Kolkata. The selection of these three different populations was primarily based on their differential positions in the continuum of marginalization in the city of Kolkata. Population I and Population II were the two 'illegal'/'non-legitimized' squatter settlements and Population III was a 'recognized'/'legitimized' slum settlement in the city of Kolkata. In the first two settlements, residents did not have any security of tenure and they were evicted from both the places during the course of this study. Population I was evicted to make the widening an existing flyover in the east central Park Circus region of Kolkata and Population II for the implementation of Ganga Action Plan under which the Beliaghata Canal (Population II was on the side to this canal in the central region of Kolkata) was to be dredged and made navigable. Population III, on the other hand, was a recognized slum where the residents were living with a kind of security of tenure as they had received *pattas* from the government (an agreement with the government which is considered as a kind of entitlement) under the provision of Calcutta Thika and Other tenancies and Land (Acquisition and Regulation) Act, 1981and had obtained the right of *Thika* Tenants from the government - a right that allowed slum-dwellers in Kolkata to live on the land and build houses but not to sell the land. In this study, Population I and Population II, collectively, were considered as the Control Group as did not receive the program of the security of tenure in their settlement. Population III was considered as the Program Group where the residents were enjoying the program of security of tenure in the form of *Thika* Tenancy for over a decade before the commencement of this work. The author hoped to carry out his research on the marginalization of population and child labor in a Third World urban situation like Kolkata within this framework.

BACKGROUND OF THE WORK

Foregrounding this study on the marginalization of population and child labor in the Third World city of Kolkata, like the other anthropological studies in urban areas, on basis of the forms and principles of our discipline was the first major problem that the author faced. This dilemma stemmed from the fact that anthropology by tradition is based on the study of kin-based societies where, unlike in complex urban scenario, all the alliances of the informant(s) can be placed on cognitive grid of kin, clan and affine. However, anthropological studies on urban issues are not that uncommon as we find numerous studies on the various aspects of urban life like migration, social networks, street-corner cliques, neighborhoods, political processes, traders and entrepreneurs, careers, patron-client relations, voluntary associations, religious congregations, public ceremonies, urban festivals, bureaucratic encounters and social movements. More holistic attempts have also been made in anthropology to elaborate forms and qualities of urbanism, rural-urban continuum, diverse heterogenetic and traditional orthogenetic urban centers, regional and transnational social orders, marketing networks, dimensions of scale and specialization, spatial symbolism, and cross-cultural domains of urban life.

Urban issues have regularly crept into the discipline in recent past and *urban anthropology* has emerged as a major sub-discipline within anthropology. This tradition began with some stalwart cultural anthropologists in USA like Redfield, Child and Sjoberg who worked extensively on different urban issues in the First World as well as in the Third World. During the late 1960s, the increasing assimilation of peasants and tribal people, the traditional target groups of the anthropologists, in the urbanized world facilitated the construction of urban anthropology around the works of Lewis, Hannerz and Southall. During the 1970s, some textbooks, readers and reviews on urban anthropology appeared, among them was the first integrated textbook on urban anthropology in 1977 by Richard Fox where he emphasized on the need for understanding the city in the context of the wider society. The distinctive features of the body of work in urban anthropology till 1970s were under the topical headings of urbanism (Fox 1977), urban subcultures (Whyte 1943, Geertz 1960, Lewis 1966) and urbanization. During 1980s and 1990s, second and third generation of more theory-oriented works on urban anthropology emerged and new discourses on the questions of development in Third World have also emerged (Castells 1983, Escobar 1988; Gugler 1988). Lately urban anthropology has been concerned with a whole gamut of issues like gender, sexuality, ethnicity etc. in urban settings along with other issues like urban politics, religion, popular culture etc. In other words, urban anthropology now has started paying increasing attention to more complicated urban issues like the needs of a heterogeneous urban population and their taste cultures. This discipline envisions that the vast on-going expansion of urban space throughout the world as a result of the accelerated urbanization would cause an uprooting of countless human beings from familiar places and create attachments to new places as the author observed in this work. The psychological, symbolic and political processes involved in this culturalization (and deculturalization) of urban space have thus become a core area of study in urban anthropology (Rodman 1992, Leeds 1994).

In India, urban anthropology as a separate sub-discipline within anthropology made a rather late arrival during the 1980s with few textbooks, reviews and other anthropological writings on Indian cities. But from the 1950s, different urban issues have been intensively studied by different social scientists including the anthropologists. Some of these works are regarded as immensely valued anthropological treasures since they are based on long-term intensive research among different ethnic, cultural groups and on diversified problems associated with urban life. These works on Indian cities include studies on urban space, continuity and change in the historical past of Indian cities, pattern of social institutions in Indian cities like marriage, kinship, neighborhood, caste, family and religion along with the studies on urban middle class, urban elite, great and little traditions in urban India and urban sacred complex in India. These works, though the often made sincere attempts to give insights into different facets of urban life, could not always explained the features of a city itself. More recently the debate on *the anthropology in cities and the anthropology of cities* (see Kemper, 1991) has become a recent entrant in our discipline. Notwithstanding these debates anthropological studies in urban areas, especially in the Third World are all set to grow rapidly and the author envisions that the acceleration of Third World urbanization will push diverse fields within anthropology towards a closer integration with this burgeoning sub-discipline.

With these introductory discussions on the work and its background the author would like to focus on the debates related with the definitions and conceptions of child labor which has been discussed in the next chapter. These debates run through the fault line associated with the debates on imperialism as many Western observers consider child labor as a menace to be eradicated with immediate effect. But, on the other hand, some observers both from the West and non-West found child labor as a "necessary evil" in poor countries such as India for the maintenance of the millions of vulnerable families. In this context, it must be mentioned here that some observers in India consider child labor as somewhat virtuous since it gives jobs to the children of millions of starving families. In fact, some academics and activists campaign not for the reduction of child labor but only for a reduction in the exploitation of children. However, the question has to be asked whether it is justifiable to allow children from the poor and vulnerable families to undergo such physical, cognitive, emotional and moral traumas because they must help their families. Is the joy of childhood reserved only for some privileged children? To answer these questions we need to create a completely different discourse on child labor which can give us a new understanding of this phenomenon.

CHAPTER 2

CONCEPTS OF CHILD LABOR: A CRITICAL REVIEW

Western scholars and their non-Western counterparts have made various attempts to conceptualize the phenomenon of child labor. All these attempts primarily revolve around the questions like -
i) What is child work? and
ii) What constitutes the difference between child work and child labor?

Most conclusions to these inquiries have been offered by the works of Western scholars, activists, and policy makers. The author found that the majority of
these workers have actually oversimplified and generalized their responses so
that what possibly serves as "child labor" in one culture may conversely be per-
ceived as "child work" in another. This is not to say that the Western world is
oblivious of the basic realities behind the prevalence of child labor problem in
the Third World. We find that Alec Fyfe observes that in child labor one needs
to decipher the difference between the issues of work and labor and he
states, "We need to make a distinction between 'child work' and 'child labor'.
This has led to much confusion as well as failure to focus and mobilize significant attention on the real priorities within the field" (Fyfe 1989: 4). Similarly,
Viviana Zelizer notes, "It is often unclear what specific occupations transformed
a child into an exploited laborer, or what determined the legitimacy of some
forms of child work" (Zelizer 1985: 73). In fact, efforts to distinguish child work
from child labor have remained by and large unsuccessful because both exist as
cultural constructions with culturally relative definitions (Zelizer 1985: 73).
The difficulty in drawing a line between child labor and a child's every day
work as well as the inter-changeability of these terms used to classify the exploitation of children through work among other issues actually allowed Western
concepts of child labor and child work to extend globally. It caused problems in
the formulation and implementation of policies in nations where child labor may
not necessarily mean the same thing as what it represents in the United States
and much of Western Europe (Fyfe 1989: 4, Boyden 1991, Szanton Blanc 1994).
Moreover, the inaccurate and vague definitions have led to a greater problem:
the inability "to reach a precise national accounting of the number of child laborers" (Zelizer 1985: 73).

Toward a Definition of Child Labor

Western scholars, activists, and politicians have formulated the predominant, yet
simultaneously ambiguous, characterization(s) of child labor. These members
from Western tradition, the majority working with such Western-based non-
governmental organizations as the United Nations Children's Fund (UNICEF),
Amnesty International, Save the Children Fund, and the International Labor Organization (ILO), have classified child labor as somehow distinct from the everyday chores of the child, jobs such as washing the dishes, cooking, milking the
cows, and taking the trash out. However, this interest in the subject of child labor, the desire to separate work from labor, and the hope to aid children in these
circumstances only became a major concern in the mid-1980s (ILO 1996: 4).
Until this emergence, "child labor was viewed with a mixture of indifference,

apathy and even cynicism. It was widely practiced and accepted by many as part of the natural order of things. For others, child labor was equated with the argument that work is good for children and a means of helping families" (ILO 1996: 4). Until recently there existed two principal views on child labor: one, that child labor was unimportant, and two, that some people or cultural norms followed that child work was a form of socialization, of teaching children their future social, political, economical, racial, and gender roles (Benedict 1955, Mead 1955, Ruark 2000, Scheper-Hughes and Sargent 1998). In some instances, it was a form of helping the family financially as a means for survival (Boyden 1991). But a larger question remained whether one should justify this phenomenon which denied childhood to the children coming from marginalized and vulnerable families on the pretext of survival of those families.

Who should be Called a Child and Why?

Gradually the question of child labor became associated with the question of 'who should be called a child and why?' In a world where approximately two hundred and fifty million children between the ages of five and fourteen, spreading across Asia, Africa, Europe, Latin America and the Caribbean (ILO 1996: 7), it is difficult to pinpoint precisely a universal definition of the child as well as childhood. The United Nations Convention on the Rights of the Child defines the child in Article 1 as "every human being below the age of eighteen years" (Stephens 1995: 336). The majority of other Western theorists and policy makers categorize children based upon the physical sciences: biology and psychology, including chronological age and physical and mental development (James, Jenks and Prout 1998). de la Luz Silva defines "child as someone who needs adult-protection for physical, psychological and intellectual development until able to become independently integrated into the adult world" (de la Luz Silva 1981: 160). Goddard and White are of the view, "its definition varies from one society and from one time to another, and also according to both class and gender" (Goddard and White 1982: 468). However, Alison James and Alan Prout do not define "the child" but ask the powerful question, "What is a child?" (James and Prout 1997: 1). Perhaps they should have asked, "What is childhood?" Instead, in *Theorizing Childhood*, Alison James, Chris Jenks, and Alan Prout note the predominant Western opinion of childhood as the period of socialization - the process in which a child trains to become an adult and learns about his or her culture and role in society (James, Jenks and Prout 1998: 23). However, "What is a child?" and "What is childhood?" remain largely unanswered in view of the many existing responses to these inquiries. The definitions of children and childhood persist as ambiguous and paradoxical because these terms are culturally constructed and defined, as well as heavily influenced by history, politics, and the economy. Discussing the matter of childhood, Ruth Benedict exclaims in *Continuities and Discontinuities in Cultural Conditioning*, "All cultures must deal in one way or another with the cycle of growth from infancy to adulthood . . . . Although it is a fact of nature that the child becomes a man, the way in which this transition is effected varies from one society to another, and no one of these particular cultural bridges should be regarded as the 'natural' path of maturity" (Mead and Wolfenstein 1955: 21). Benedict's conclusion relates to Sharon Stephen's statement that, "Each culture defines childhood in terms of its own set of meanings and practices" (Stephens 1995: 8). Therefore, the child and childhood exist as cultural constructions, and each must be examined in light of the history, politics, economics, and social structures within which they fall. This is to say that Western characterizations of the realities of children and childhood cannot be applied cross-culturally.

The author should also add here that even within India the child has been defined differently from state to state for different sets of legislation. The Acts, which have been formulated to prevent the exploitation of the young, define a child as a person under 18 years in Gujarat and West Bengal, under 16 years in Madhya Pradesh, Uttar Pradesh and Punjab, under 16 years in Telengana region but under 14 years in rest of Andhra Pradesh. In the Union Territories, a boy is a child if he is under 16 years and a girl if she is under 18 years. It is not only easier for numerical and comparative measures to define a child up to the age of 14 years (as the universally accepted method of dividing age-groups is grouping them in intervals of 5 years i.e. 0-4, 5-9, 10-14 and so on), it is also a fact that the full time participation in the economic activity below this age is in a violation of Article 45 (see below) and Article 24 (see below) of the Constitution of India.

What is Labor/Labor Force/Work?

Another dimension of this problem is associated with the nature of labor/labor force/work linked with child labor. According to UN "the working population consists of those individuals who take part in the production of economic goods and services, including unpaid family workers in an economic enterprise as well as persons who work for pay or profit" (United Nations 1958: 22-23). According to ILO "All persons of either sex who furnish the supply of production of economic goods and services as defined by the United Nations accounts and balances" (ILO 1982). This definition of "economic" (and therefore labor force) activity is very broad, since it is based on the United Nations system of national income account statistics (i.e. SNA) definition of "economic" goods and services. "According to these systems [of national accounts], the production of economic goods and services should include all production and processing of primary products, whether for the market, for barter for own consumption" (ILO 1982).

The Census of India defines work as "participation in any economically productive activity. Such participation may be physical or mental in nature. Work involves not only active work but also effective supervision and direction of work" (RGI 1981: 2). de la Luz Silva observes that in the case of children "'work' often straddles the borderline between work and play, work and vagrancy, and work and apprenticeship. Apprenticeship is a second highly important element it may contribute to children's socialization and acquisition of technical skills, but when it is simply a device to obtain cheap labor, 'apprenticeship' hinders future development. This element highlights the specific kind of exploitation inherent in child work, which is additional to the direct exploitation also experienced by adults entering the productive system in similar fashion" (de la Luz Silva 1981: 164). According to Morice, "a definition of work should be related not only to the activity itself but also to its economic and social context" (Morice 1981: 136), i.e. the exploitative and non-exploitative nature should also be taken into consideration. In a little different vein, Goddard and White observes, "The phenomenon of child labor encompasses both (biologically) juvenile workers doing 'adult' work and (biological) adults who are still defined in work-relations as minors (trainees, apprentices, helpers, unmarried or young married workers in a parental farm or other enterprise, etc.) and thus subject to various forms of exploitation and loss of autonomy which 'social' adults do not face" (Goddard and White 1982: 468). Schildkrout has given a possible working definition of children's work as "any activity done by children, which either contributes to production, gives adults free time, facilitates the work of others, or substitutes for the employment of others" (Schildkrout 1981: 95). Bekombo, on the other hand, opines that the definition of work or employment is based largely on the volume and destination of the product of child's activities. He feels that "far from invariably implying *exploitation*, the work of children can be, according to cultural context, an expression of an educational principle according to which, if only in *anticipation*, each individual makes a sacrifice to the community who, then, accepts him or her as a member" (Bekembo 1981: 121).

Some even support child labor and employ children because hiring a child costs less than employing an adult. In fact, some of the work kids perform is unwaged, free labor (US Department of Labor 1995). One view in favor of child labor is that the child's skills are irreplaceable following the "nimble fingers' argument" (ILO 1996: 18). This is to say that a child's small physique allows him or her to carry out specific tasks that an adult's much larger bodily structure cannot i.e. "only children with small fingers have the ability to make fine hand-knotted carpets" (ILO 1996: 18). While the exact reasons why children work and why they are employed vary, the most important reasons follow that "children are less aware of their rights, less troublesome and more willing to take orders and to do monotonous work without complaining (indeed, children often engage in work activities which are considered too menial by many adults), more trustworthy, less likely to steal, and less likely to be absent from work" (ILO 1996: 20); also, "[children] can be made to do jobs that adults find degrading or unpleasant" (Boyden 1991: 123). Singh et al. in this context observes "Labor in case of the child, especially, is harmful because the energy that should have been spent on the nurturing of his latent powers is consumed for purposes of his survival. Thus child labor assumes the character of a social problem in as much as it hinders, arrests or distorts the natural growth processes and prevents the child from attaining his full blown manhood" (Singh et al. 1980: 1-2). Premature hard labor by children not only reduces their physical vigor and energy but aggravates defects and ailments in them also, e.g., throat and lung infections, cardiac weakness, nervous problems and so on. It has also been observed that the child labor is "economically unsound, psychologically disastrous and physically as well as morally dangerous and harmful" (Singh et al. 1980: 9). Therefore, the growing concern for the world's working children stemmed with the realization that certain forms of child work and conditions under which children labored were exploitative and abusive to the children, constituting a form of slavery (ILO 1996: 4).

Need for Culturally Relative Definitions

The lack of culturally relative assessments of children in and of child labor connects with the inabilities of policy makers to help mitigate this harsh reality which deny childhood to a huge share of humanity. Western policy makers and non-governmental organizations face a problem when they attempt to apply their own policies formulated on the Western definitions of child labor and child exploitation in non-Western cultures where characterizations and the means to formulate and implement laws differ. In fact, this lack of culturally specific analyses often leave children in situations far worse than what one can imagine i.e. their childhoods are spent as child domestic workers, street children, prostitutes, cigarette rollers, or bricklayers without being noticed. As an anthropologist the author finds it absolutely imperative to (re)examine on an urgent basis the whole of a culture—class, race, economics, and politics—as well as the culturally constructed and relative definitions and perceptions of child labor in order to create new solutions, which not only aim at eradicating the child labor, but also seek to improve the opportunities available throughout the world. In the next section the author explains why this (re)examination has become essential today to solve the problem of child labor in the Third World countries.

Toward a New Concept of Child Labor?

Although the meaning of child labor is still paradoxical both in regard to exploitative and non-exploitative work, although it exists as a reality within many of the world's cultural traditions particularly in the Third World countries like India, for a variety of reasons, including politics, the global market economy, and rural to urban migration (Boyden 1991). This work on child labor in a Third World urban situation has examined various aspects of this paradox and the pivotal role that anthropology can play in analyzing the phenomenon of child labor in the contemporary rapidly evolving global scenario.

Anthropological researches focus on the global predicament of child labor and the exploitation of children in the labor market also remain crucial (Boyden 1991, Nieuwenhuys 1996, Szanton Blanc 1994). Similarly the quest for ways of eliminating child labor has remained central to the concerns of anthropologists associated with various national and international agencies as well as non-governmental organizations (ILO 1996, UNICEF 2000, Szanton Blanc 1994) worldwide. Existing accounts assess children's agency as producers and consumers in a capitalistic order through the labors they perform (Hendrick 1997: James, Jenks, and Prout 1998, Nieuwenhuys 1996, Stephens 1995, Szanton Blanc 1994, Zelizer 1985). In fact, these anthropological contributions to the issue of child labor are very important as they bring into light children's importance, the significance of children's work and abilities, and their involvement in the local and global system (Mintz 1977, Nieuwenhuys 1996, Stephens 1995, Szanton-Blanc 1994). Through these accounts it became increasingly clear that children's work is not merely "socialization, education, training, [or] play," (Nieuwenhuys 1996: 237) but rather a vital contribution to the world around them.

While anthropological assessments have emphasized the lack of a universal definition of "child labor" because the meanings are culturally constructed and relative, therefore affirming the difficulty in implementing a universal model to be used to combat these exploitative conditions of the world's disadvantaged children (James, Jenks, and Prout 1998), they have also expanded the scope of children's work and children's worth within a capitalist system. However, the discipline has yet to conduct culturally relative examinations comprehensively through ethnography of the physical, emotional, and sexual abuses children face, the impact this has on their lives, and the child's own opinions about his or her position as a child laborer (Ruark 2000). Also, the social, political, and economic inequalities that lead to the continual practice of exploitative child work are yet to be properly explored. These anthropological works have, similar to those compositions of non-governmental organizations and policy makers, made generalizations when assessing child labor, talking about the situation around the world (Boyden 1991, James, Jenks, and Prout 1998) and not child labor in the Third World countries like India as individual nations with their own constructions of the child, the childhood, and the child labor. Many have failed to explain how these factors are played out through specific forms of work and analyze the variations that exist from country to country, culture to culture. Most of the anthropological works have examined the global without exploring the local (Mintz 1977). This work found that though the global scenario is responsible for child labor situation, the local situation in the Third World is equally important for the creation of child labor and must also be studied thoroughly to get a complete picture on this problem.

Methodological Considerations on the Cause of Child Labor

There is no consensus among the academics and the researchers on the methodological issues related with child labor. There are different causes of child labor cited by different observers. Some of these causes are discussed briefly here.

Factors at the Household Level: There are a number of factors at the household level that can determine whether a child is to be sent to work, either around the household or away from the household. At the core of this debate the household has various members whose time is divided among various tasks which determines this decision. On the other hand, the decision to send children to school is definitely observed as a 'deferred investment' that incurs costs in the present and yields benefits in the future. Whether a household would be prepared to incur this cost is dependent on several issues related to the condition of the household. The author would like to mention some of these issues here.

i) Issues related to the economic condition of the household: Most observers believe that the impoverished parents send their children to work in order to supplement the family income (Grootaert and Kanbur 1995, Basu and Van 1998, Ahmed 1999). In a word, there is a virtual unanimity among the observers that poverty is the main, although not the only, cause of child labor. This means if households do not have enough money to meet basic needs, children are more likely to work and less likely to be sent to school for education. Poverty also implies an inability to be able to afford to send a child to school as education (primary, secondary and higher secondary) is not free in many countries though in the province of West Bengal in India where this fieldwork was done, the primary, secondary and higher secondary educations are free in the state-owned and state-aided institutions. Again, if education yielded very high returns in the form of higher future earnings for the child, and if there could be a way to enforce loan contracts, in principle households could borrow money to finance current consumption and costs of education, which could then be repaid out of future earnings of the child. In most wealthy countries, this form of financing is used for higher education as the parents take educational loans for the higher education of their children which the children repay when they start earning. It can be argued that the individuals realize that education is a worthwhile investment with high returns, and since they may not be able to afford to pay for higher education directly, they borrow against their future earnings in the form of student loans in order to finance the investment. Of course, markets for such loans for a cross-section of people rarely exist in most of the Third World countries like India and there are virtually no such facilities for the poor and marginalized people. Findings suggest that if the households do not have enough cash on hand to send their children to school, but education is viewed as worthwhile, often one child may be sent to work in order to help finance the education of their siblings (Jensen 1999).

The notion of vulnerability due to income instability and spiraling debt of the households is also critical in thinking about the factors that determine whether children would work (Jensen 1999, 2000). This is due to the fact that if households cannot save or borrow in credit markets, they must finance all consumption and investments in children (including education) out of current income and such investments can be quite costly considering the paltry income that these families generate. If income falls in a given period, so too may consumption and investment in children, and it may become necessary to send children to work in order to meet basic needs. Income shortfalls due to the income instability could also lead to households incurring debt, especially from money lenders or local merchants or craftsmen. And such debt in itself could be a cause of child labor. In many Third World countries including India, a part of the debt is repaid by assigning the child to the lender as an indentured laborer (Baland and Robinson 2000).

ii) Issues related to the family composition and perception on the children: According to the observers the most important issue related to the composition of the family is its size. If households have limited income then having more children means a smaller investment in each child. Thus households with more children end up providing less education for each child and may need to send children to work to help augment family income. Other relevant point of this issue is the sex composition of the household as in India like many other Third World countries educating a girl is a lower priority than educating a boy. If the returns for education for boys are higher than for girls, they typically are higher for boys - a reflection of discrimination against women in the labor market - then the parents with limited resources are likely to invest first in those children who give the highest returns. This may mean that girls may lose out to boys in preference from their own families. It can further be noted that for a given child, their level of education could depend on not just the number of siblings they have, but also on the sex-composition of the number of siblings (Butcher and Case 1994, Garg and Morduch 1998 and Morduch 2000).

Parental lack of motivation to send their children to schools is another major cause of child labor. If the parents do not perceive that education yields returns, they most likely would not send their children to school. This may either due to the absence of literacy among the parents and/or the parents may not view the school curriculum as relevant to their children's future, either because it does not teach them practical skills, or perhaps they prefer, say, female children get married early rather than have a career which requires education. In fact, education in some cultures in South Asia is seen to make daughters 'less marriageable'. However, some studies indicate that parents who have achieved a higher level of education are also more likely to ensure that their children receive a good education (Basu and Tzannatos 2003).

Factors beyond the Household Level: The individual households have little or no control over on several factors related to child labor.

i) Demand for child labor: This argument basically revolves round the constructions of demand-supply in labor market. It is a fact that there is a huge demand for child labor by employers in the informal as well as few formal enterprises in the Third World which is driven by the need to maximize profit. Children are preferred than their adult counterparts by these employers as laborers for various reasons like low wage (sometimes employers do not pay anything in the pretext of apprenticeship), non-wage benefits (such as medical insurance or pensions are virtually non-existent), better obedience of orders etc. Working children may also be less likely to demand better conditions or capable of working longer, which may allow the employers to keep production costs lower. Some observers believe that the children perform tasks that adults are supposedly unable to perform (Bachman 2000), such as working in small, cramped areas (like mine tunnels), or weaving more intricate knots and patterns in carpets (so-called 'nimble fingers' argument). This argument has been rebuffed by various observers like

Levison et al. (1996) whose study shows that there is no evidence that children in the carpet industry of Uttar Pradesh are more productive than adults. Instead, children, hired on lower wages, are more likely to work on low-quality carpets. However, employing children also depresses the wage rate for the adult workers which benefit the employers.

ii) National and international initiatives on child labor: Various national and international efforts have been undertaken by different agencies to solve the problem of child labor throughout the world. We find that in the Third World countries (including India) several official reports, constitutional safeguards, legal provisions and other national and international initiatives on child labor. These international initiatives include international pressure to comply with labor standards and regulations, foreign and international laws regarding the import of products made using child labor, and pressure from the advocacy and the interest groups. These efforts were initiated to protect the children particularly from the strenuous jobs. These initiatives can also affect the child labor situation in various ways. In one such study in Bangladesh Bissell (2004) has shown that due to an initiative from the US government and the entrepreneurs Bangladeshi textile exporters, to protect their trade, began to fire children, and ultimately around 40,000 children, mainly young girls, became worse off than before as they lost their only source of income. Another study on carpet industry in India (Sharma et al. 2000) has revealed that though the incidence of child labor in core carpet belt has declined due to various national and international initiatives, children who were working in carpet industry have now shifted to other occupations such as sari-weaving, beedi-making, road-side hotels and agriculture.

iii) Cultural contexts of child labor: Being an anthropologist, the author naturally emphasized on the study of the cultural and social attitudes toward children and child labor as these attitudes are important determinants for its creation and continuation. Traditionally in the Indian subcontinent work is considered a part of socialization for children. Guru-Shishya Parampara (the tradition of direct training from the Gurus to the trainees) has remained deep-rooted in the culture of Indian subcontinent. Under this tradition Guru teaches lessons, ranging from the scriptures to various practical trainings, to his Shishyas (trainees) from a tender age. In return the trainees give services to their guru. In such a context, child labor is not to be shunned but sometimes even reinforced by the insipid and non-rewarding nature of modern educational system. Thus the tendency of the parents to send their children for apprenticeship for a skilled work to a master craftsman/mechanic is a legacy of the past cultural practices of the subcontinent.

iv) Globalization, marginalization and child labor problem: Anthropologists from different parts of the world have studied on the global predicament of child labor and the exploitation of children in the labor market (Boyden 1991, Nieuwenhuys 1996, Szanton Blanc 1994) and the involvement of child labor in the local and global system (Mintz 1977, Nieuwenhuys 1996, Stephens 1995, Szanton-Blanc 1994, Lieten and White 2001, Lieten 2002). Present studies on child labor need to consider various international factors like international trade and globalization, international pressures to comply with labor standards and regulations and impact of Structural Adjustment Programs (SAP) on child labor in the Third World countries as the world has become more integrated than ever.

The opinions on the effects of globalization on child labor are varied and sometimes diametrically opposite to each other. According to the proponents of globalization trade liberalization in a developing country, which is abundant in unskilled labor, will not only have a substitution but an income effect also. Even if it is assumed that the liberalized trade does not raise the growth of the general economy in the developing countries, it will raise the relative rate of return of unskilled labor which reduces the incentive for parents with little skills to send their children to work (see Basu and Van 1998, Basu 2002, Becker 1997). Other proponents of globalization argue that the more open countries are likely to have lower interest rates and offer better access to credit which should lower the opportunity of the cost of education and thereby the incidence of child labor (see Ranjan 2001, Jafarey and Lahiri 2002). Others in this camp think that an open economy is less likely to preserve the traditional culture and institutional framework that promotes child labor (Shelburne 2001, Aggarwal 1995). It has further been argued that globalization with its attendant revolution in the form of information and communications cannot let the cases of child abuses go unreported particularly in the cities. Thus the foreign investors who find it difficult to circumvent anti-child labor laws from various regulators are more likely to join different labeling institutions which are meant for reducing child labor as it gives them positive publicity (Spar 1998, McClintock 1999).

According to the opponents of globalization, free market in developing countries, which are abundant in unskilled labor, creates a hunt for cheap labor in the form of child labor. The altered role of the state preventing it to act as a buffer will also result in rise in the relative rate of return to unskilled labor and reduce the incentive to invest in skills and education. As a consequence, the returns to child labor increase with a substitution effect toward increased supply of child labor (Grootaert and Kanbur 1995). In fact, Cornia et al. (1988) state that increases in the number of child laborers and school drop-outs have more immediate consequences of the crisis. Specifically in India these increases have resulted in an overall increase in social and economic insecurity which puts extreme pressure on the ability of poor families to cope and survive economic hardship. Besides, the expansion of the informal economy operates, both indirectly and directly, to the increase of child labor in various ways. The expansion of the informal economy (wherein labor intensive processes requiring lower level skills are farmed out) has led to an increase in women working under onerous conditions to eke out a livelihood. This has invariably meant that the children also start working with their mothers or do various domestic chores to relieve their mothers for work outside the home. More importantly, the subsidiaries of multinational corporations sub-contract part of their production to small firms which rely heavily on child labor. Even large export-oriented enterprises resort to similar sub-contracting to small firms which engage child laborers. Sometimes there are more direct correlations of child labor with the SAP as under this, many countries receive loans from the World Bank/IMF only conditional on impose school fees among other things in order to assure international organizations that the recipient nation is conducting that they sound and responsible fiscal policy. Several countries in Africa, for example Uganda, had to impose these fees, which had been non-existent since its independence. An immediate consequence of each of these measures in the pretext of fiscal austerity is that many children from the families in chronic poverty may be prevented from attending school and driven to child labor in the ill-paid, back-breaking informal sector of economy (also see Kearney 2001, Maskus 1997, Palley 2002, Rodrik 1996).

If we examine the Indian census data on child labor (though the census data and National Sample Survey data on child labor have repeatedly been accused of giving undercounts) in the context of globalization (see Appendix I for a statewise distribution of working children according to 1971, 1981, 1991 and 2001) we can find a steady increase in the number of working children except during the period between 1981 and 1991. Even during the last decade during when India jumped onto the bandwagon of globalization, the number of child laborers increased from 11.28 million to 12.67 million. Some states like Maharashtra and Punjab which went all-out for trade liberalization have in fact experienced an increase in the number of child labor.

Globalization also intensifies the phenomenon of urban marginalization caused by the inability of market economy to provide adequate shelter and urban services to an increasing proportion of city dwellers. This phenomenon of urban marginalization is not always synonymous with occupational marginalization. Occupational marginalization, in contrast, occurs due to the uneven capitalist development combined with a disintegration of existing productive forms which is not matched by the creation of new sources of employment. These are the basic dynamics of the so-called 'informal' economy which leads to occupational marginalization. But differential distribution of the collective consumption (i.e. state provided and/or mediated basic amenities) or more precisely the lack of access to collective consumption is regarded as symptomatic of urban marginalization. In spite of every argument on the restrictiveness of social provision to spatial references, the primeval role of struggle over urban space in this differential distribution is incontestable. The author found during this study that the boundaries in urban spaces are selectively permeable: various people are admitted to or excluded from, various spatial domains or settings and may penetrate deeply or just minimally, may become central or controlling or remain peripheral, depending on who they are, and what rules apply. This is likely to vary over time as people typically excluded may be allowed to cross boundaries and enter spatial domains at certain times (Suttles 1968). Thus different spaces in an urban area appear. Some of these spaces are meant for *personal occupancy* (e.g. the dwelling) with strictest restrictions for admission, *community occupancy* (e.g. a private club) with restrictions within defined limits, *society occupancy* (e.g. a street) where restrictions to the non-members apply and *free occupancy* where no restriction is applicable. During this fieldwork the author found that two such urban spaces meant for personal occupancy for a group of urban marginal people were transformed to the urban space meant for society occupancy for another group of urban dwellers and this transformation rendered those urban marginal people homeless.

The author has found from his long fieldwork experiences in Kolkata that the forces of globalization create a huge proportion of marginalized people in the Third World cities as the state's roll back system results in a failure to provide adequate collective consumption (urban basic services) to an increasing proportion of the urban population. Again the cities act as the facilitators of globalization in Third World countries and the cities in these countries are gearing up to become 'global' cities with some modern facilities for its 'legitimate' inhibitors. In this process the 'illegitimate' dwellers in squatters and slums are sometimes getting forcefully evicted which create a new cycle of vulnerability and produce more child laborers in the Third World cities. The neo-liberal economic policy, which has become the official economic policy of globalization in every single country was replaced all the old policies of protection of national industries (like import-substitution, production licenses and import tariffs) and its citizens (like food subsidies, free health services, subsidized education system, employment-guarantee program, income-redistribution policies, several protection policies for the old, women and children). All these have increased marginalization as well as vulnerability of the citizens in the Third World countries and created conditions in which child labor has become a survival strategy for the marginal families in the Third World cities.

Dealing With the Child Labor Problem

Opinions also vary on the ways of dealing with the problem of child labor. By and large these viewpoints can be fitted into three different camps.

i) *The Non-Interventionists:* This viewpoint argues that there are underlying structural problems of poverty, underdevelopment and high fertility that cause child labor. Child labor is a symptom of these problems and is a mechanism through which households cope with chronic poverty. As long as poverty persists, removing children from certain particular industries, though well-intentioned, may push them into even more degrading forms of child labor, such as prostitution. Further, these households depend on the income from their children, and the loss of this income could bring adverse consequences, perhaps as bad as child labor itself. If poverty is a cause of low school enrolment, forcing children out of work will not mean that they will be able to afford schooling, and in fact may be less able to do so. This viewpoint also claims that the international pressure to act against child labor, such as product bans or labeling, are more often the voices of powerful, protectionist labor interests within developed nations. Further, there is little evidence that convention, decree or law will in itself reduce or eliminate child labor (Brown, Christainsen and Philips 1992, Moehling 1999). According to this camp, the best way to get children to go to school and out of the factories is by economic incentives as unless individuals see incentives for going to school and not work, they will not be prepared to do it. Without proper and targeted economic growth and/or change as well as availability of jobs that reward education, parents will not send kids to school. Besides, outright bans do not seem to work, because the larger problem is the enforcement in Third World situations like India where millions work in the informal economy.

ii) The Abolitionists: According to this approach, the consequences of child labor are so damaging that only an outright ban is appropriate. The best approach, according to the abolitionists, is to enforce school enrolment rather than minimum work age, because it is easier to monitor school attendance rather than check every factory and home for whether children work. There is evidence that even with economic growth child labor is often not reduced (Swaminatan 1999). Child labor is considered as a 'bad equilibrium,' and a ban can become self-enforcing (Basu and Van 1998). This argument states that if there is a ban on child labor, the resulting decline in total labor supply would lead to an increase in adult wages, and that the corresponding increase in adult wages would mean that households would no longer want to send their children to work. There is evidence that the compulsory schooling laws did have an effect in the US on increasing school enrolment rates, and have played a decisive role in the long-term decline of child labor (Margo and Aldrich 1996).

iii) The Non-radicals: This view holds that there should a long-term goal of eliminating child labor but in the short-run resources must be devoted wholly to minimize the adverse impacts of child labor. Researchers of this viewpoint argue that there are underlying structural problems that cause child labor. However, the consequences are sufficiently dire, especially for the worst forms of child labor in hazardous conditions (see Appendix II) that it is worth trying to reduce it. But in doing so one should relentlessly try to minimize the effect of lost income (also see ILO 1998: 107-108). Focusing on improving workplace conditions, reducing injuries and hours, allowing children to combine work with schooling, improving school quality and encouraging school attendance, and attempting to stimulate adult employment to minimize income loss to households, while working on policies to ultimately reduce and eliminate child labor altogether.

Thus, one can find that the existing concepts on child labor fail to explain the child labor situation adequately particularly in Third World urban situation. The reason of this failure can be found from the fact that child labor is predominantly a Third World affair and the prevalent concepts have some Western presence in it. Thus a search for an alternative discourse in this regard for a Third Worldly understanding on this issue has become urgently needed now. The author would now like to discuss the magnitude of the problem of child labor and the national and international initiatives against child labor. Along with this discussion the author has also described the results of his decade-long field study among the marginalized communities and the problem of child labor among those people in the city of Kolkata. These discussions will give the readers an idea on the nature and magnitude of the problem as well as the need for a change in direction of thought regarding child labor as without this shift the child labor situation in the Third World would not change.

CHAPTER 3

TOWARD A NEW UNDERSTANDING OF CHILD LABOR IN THE URBAN THIRD WORLD

With the advent of globalization and its attendant free movement of capital and national labor we are witnessing a huge demographic transition toward the major urban areas in the traditional Third World countries like India. These migrants to the cities are taking refuge in the ill-paid unskilled informal economy and releasing their children for work which resulted in an unprecedented proliferation of child labor. With this exceptional level of urbanization it is predicted that in the near future more than half of the Third World population will live in the cities. It is also projected that by 2015, about 60 cities will have more than 5 million people (overwhelming majority of these cities will be in the Third World) and the Third World megacities like Mumbai, Mexico City, Lagos, Karachi and Kolkata are expected to reach an urban population of more than 20 million (UNCHS 2001b). It is the Third World in the global South which is testing the waters for what the future of urbanization might look like and this trend challenges the dominant Western -mostly Eurocentric- image of urban life. As a part of this challenge the phenomenon of child labor in the Third World cities like Kolkata has to be revisited with a Third Worldly understanding of this phenomenon. The author argues that since child labor is predominantly a Third World phenomenon, a researcher from Third World background rather than one from Western background would be better positioned to create such an understanding. He further argues that anthropology with its special focus on micro-level ethnographic study has always formed a unique tool in bringing out actor's own view on the reality which always helped them in bringing out an indigenous perception on the problem. Given that the discipline is a relatively new entrant in the field of urban research particularly in the Third World countries and is still trying to assume a coherent form, this work is an effort in this direction.

Background of the Study

In his pursuit toward a Third Worldly understanding of the phenomenon of child labor in a Third World urban situation, the author started this fieldwork among the marginalized people in the city of Kolkata in early 1990s – a period when India formally entered into the GATT/WTO regime – and continued till the early years of next decade when India was 'successfully' integrated with the world economy.

During this field the author found that due to the unleashing of the forces of globalization, Third World cities like Kolkata, which have become the primary destinations of capital, are experiencing rapid development. But this fast pace of development left an overwhelming proportion of the urban population 'excluded'. These 'excluded' marginalized people are living in the urban conditions where life itself is in jeopardy. In Kolkata like many other Third World cities these marginalized people make their homes on the lands which are most unsuitable for human occupation - heavily polluted and exposed to water submerging/flooding, natural hazards such as earthquakes and the dangers attaching to technological development (also see UNCHS 1996, 2001a, 2001b). The city of Kolkata, like the most Third World cities, is densely dotted by the spontaneous self-help makeshift settlements with grossly inadequate and sometimes almost non-existent urban basic amenities. Such settlements are temporarily built on useless (!) urban land.

The city of Kolkata has also been jumped onto the bandwagon of becoming a 'global' city – a facilitator of globalization. This compulsion has led different urban agencies in Kolkata to give priority to upgrade urban services and environmental conditions to make the city a better place for attracting national and international investments. This shift in policy has actually led to a progressive erosion of some 'illegal' squatter settlements from the landscape of Kolkata resulting in forced evictions in various parts of the city (COHRE 2003). During this decade-long study the author witnessed the extinction of the two settlements he studied from the landscape of Kolkata - one to widen a road and the other to dredge a canal to improve the environment of the city. These acts are resulting in further marginalization of the already 'non-included' people in the city (Bagchi 2004, 2005). These people are not only joining in the ill-paid and ruthlessly hard informal economy but they are also releasing their own children for work – a condition potentially harmful for these children and their future.

Concepts on Child Labor

A critical review of the *concepts of child labor* had put this work in proper Third World perspective. While any culturally relative definition of child labor still eludes the researchers, the author argues that the most generic characterizations on this problem follow that it is the "work which impairs the health and development of children" (Fyfe, 1989: 4) and "a denial of the right to education and of the opportunity to reach full physical and psychological development" (ILO, 1996: 8). On a thorough examination of the existing definitions author found that the term "child labor" today has become somewhat pejorative and it differs from the broader and less value-laden "child work". Child labor in general refers to the children under 14 years of age who work in both the formal and informal sectors, in conditions that are harmful or potentially harmful to the children. Underpayment of children for their work and other forms of exploitation, are also included in this definition. The author also found that the concepts on the nature of child labor vary and disagreements among the observers run very deep. As already mentioned, one view of child labor treats education as the fundamental human right for every child between the age of 5 and 14 years and holds that any child below the age of 14 who is out of school should be treated as a working child. These observers believe that the state must be held accountable for the provision of free and compulsory education to its citizens. The failure to fulfill this obligation results in a vicious poverty cycle since child labor induces poverty and poverty induces child labor. Some other researchers think that the magnitude of the problem is so enormous that it is almost impossible for the state to eradicate child labor overnight. They advocate a gradual, sequential, and selective approach toward this problem. According to this view, we should first concentrate on the release and rehabilitation of those children who are employed in hazardous occupations/processes. Subsequently we must focus on the rehabilitation of the children who are working in non-hazardous occupations. According to them, elimination of child labor by law is not possible and, they therefore, advocate a dual approach of prohibition and regulation. Still others believe that both the civil society and the state as the agents of the society have abjectly failed in making education a fundamental human right, creating the appropriate infrastructure and environment, providing incentives to ensure access to educational opportunities for all, and creating a positive and conducive school environment that will enable universal retention and participation of children who have enrolled themselves in school and also make it possible for them to achieve at least a minimum level of learning. They advocate that it should be left to the children themselves to decide whether or not they want to go to school. If the children find that the educational system (even if it is made available to them) is dull, demotivating, and irrelevant, and prefer to work, the state on behalf of the civil society should create employment opportunities that are compatible with their physical and mental capabilities.

Thus there is no one likely cause of child labor, nor can any single model adequately explain such a complex phenomenon – an argument corroborated by this study. At the most basic level, it is considered that households make decisions regarding how children's time will be allocated between leisure, schooling, household activities (chores and activities related to household economic activity) and employment. So households should be the cynosures of study when a researcher wants to research on child labor as a child without a family is inconceivable in a traditional society like India. However, the key here is not to consider the household in isolation, but to realize that decisions are made within a certain context, and are influenced by factors external to the household. Thus, beyond the household, one should consider various factors like the level of marginality of the households, schooling environment, the demand for child labor, the legal and cultural context, and the international factors like the effects of globalization. The ultimate determinants of child labor are a complex interaction among various factors acting at different levels. But we need more data from actual field situations which would consider both the culturally relative components and other factors associated with this problem. As the problem of child labor is predominantly a Third World phenomenon we need a new understanding of this problem that is sensitive to the Third World conditions because the existing concepts so far failed to grasp adequately the complexity of this problem.

Magnitude of the Problem

The question of the *magnitude of the problem of child labor* has also been no less contentious. The ILO has estimated that in the developing countries alone, 120 million children (mainly in Asia and Africa) aged between 5 and 14 are involved in full-time work, and that work is a secondary activity for another 130 million children. The number of child laborers engaged in different occupations in India has always been a bone of contention between the Government of India or government sponsored institutions and independent observers. One such official estimation, prepared by the Central Labor Ministry of the Government of India, puts the number of child labor at 17.0 million in 1992-93. The same report says that each year there is a .5 million decrease in the quantum of child labor in India. However, Indian Government has been criticized many times by ILO, latest occasion being the recent 2001 Phuket ILO meeting, for its effort to conceal the true magnitude of the country's child labor problem.

Major Child Labor Intensive Occupations in India

In India there are many occupations where child labors are employed in high numbers. Major child labor-intensive occupations in India are described as follows (also see Dingwaney 1988):

   i.   *Match and Fire Works* in Sivakasi (Tamil Nadu) employing 50,000 to 80,000 children.
   ii.   *Stone quarries* in Kerala, Markapur (Andhra Pradesh), and Mandsaur (Madhya Pradesh) employing about 20,000 children.
   iii.   *Mines* in Meghalaya employing about 28,000 children.
   iv.   *Fishing* in Kerala employing about 20,000 children.
   v.   *Handloom* in Trivandrum employing about 10,000 children.
   vi.   *Hosiery* in Tirupur (Tamil Nadu) employing about 25,000 to 35,000 children.
   vii.   *Carpet Weaving* in Jammu and Kashmir, Bhadoi, Varanasi and Mirzapur (Uttar Pradesh) employing about 2,00,000 children.
   viii.   *Pottery Making* in Kashmir and Mirzapur as well as Khurja (Uttar Pradesh) employing about 5,000 children.
   ix.   *Glass Article Making* in Firozabad (Uttar Pradesh) employing about 50,000 children.
   x.   *Gem Polishing* in Jaipur (Rajasthan) employing about 13,000 children.
   xi.   *Beedi Industries* in Nizamabad District (Andhra Pradesh), North Arcot District (Tamil Nadu) and Gujarat employing about 45,000 children.
   xii.   *Brassware Industry* in Moradabad (Uttar Pradesh) employing about 50,000 children.
   xiii.   *Diamond Industry* in Surat City (Gujarat) employing about 2, 00,000 children.
   xiv.   *Leather Units* of Agra and Kanpur (Uttar Pradesh), Durg (Madhya Pradesh) and Tonk (Rajasthan) employing about 62,000 children.

All these major child labor affected sectors are there for long period in India. These sectors along with the other child labor affected occupations have received the attention from the Indian government since the British rule. Following are the descriptions of the several official reports as well as commissions, laws and national and international initiatives on child labor in India.

According to some observers, the situation of child labor in recent time has worsened in the cities of the Third World as a result of the policies related to the structural adjustment programs (SAP) with teeming millions are pouring to the cities from the rural areas after having lost their livelihoods the children of these vulnerable section of population are swelling the pool of child laborers. It must also be mentioned here that the atmosphere of overall insecurity, which has been endemic in the Indian social scene, which has been identified as the root cause of child labor during this fieldwork and it has only further intensified with the introduction of the 'reform' under SAP (Dev 1996).

National and International Initiatives

From the pre-independence period the Indian government has formed many *commissions and committees on child labor* like Labor Investigation Committee (1946), National Commission on Labor (1969), Harbans Singh Committee (1977), Committee on Child Labor (1979) and Committee on Child Labor in Indian Industries (1981). These commissions/committees made several observations as well as recommendations and most of which were accepted by the government but those measures achieved very limited success in this regard. There are several *constitutional safeguards* in the Indian Constitution in different articles to tackle the problem of child labor.

i.   Article 23 - Prohibition of traffic in human beings and forced labor
ii.   Article 24 - Prohibition of employment of children in factories etc.
iii.   Article 39(e) and 39(f) - Certain principles of policy to be followed by state
iv.   Article 41 - The right to work, to education and to public assistance in particular circumstances
v.   Article 45 - Provision for free and compulsory education for children
vi.   Article 47 - Responsibility of the state to raise the nutritional levels, and standards of living of its citizens and to improve public health

However, these safeguards have so-far proved to be rather inadequate in dealing with the problem of child labor in India.

Government of India has also framed *several legal provisions* dating from the pre-independence period to deal with the problem of child labor. The most recent and possibly the most comprehensive of these legislations is the Child Labor (Prohibition and Regulation) Act of 1986 under which government has prohibited the employment of children in dangerous and hazardous industries and services and regulated their engagement and working conditions in non-hazardous jobs. Employers found offending this law can be punished with 3 to 12 months of rigorous imprisonment or a fine of up to 20,000 rupees or both. This law has also proved to be inadequate due to various conceptual, definitional as well as operational gaps and omissions in the existing law and these inadequacies have been exploited by various unscrupulous employers of the child labor. The Supreme Court of India passed a landmark judgment in 1996 to give more teeth to this law. The new provisions to prevent child labor in the hazardous occupations include a payment of Rs. 20,000/- by the offending employers for every child laborer employed, giving alternative employment to an adult member of the family in place of the withdrawn child laborer or payment of an amount of Rs. 5000/- for each child labor by the appropriate government, payment of interest on the corpus of Rs. 25,000/- (collected from the employers and government) to the family of the child withdrawn from the work, provision of education to the child withdrawn from the work and constitution of a separate cell in the Labor Department of Indian government for the purpose of monitoring. There have been some *other national initiatives* on behalf of the government to abolish or minimize the child labor. National Child Labor Policy, announced in 1987, is one such important effort. This policy seeks to emphasize effective enforcement of the relevant laws like Child Labor (Prohibition and Regulation) Act, 1986, the Factories Act, 1948; the Mines Act, 1952, the Plantation Labor Act, 1951 etc. The government has also undertaken some general development programs for benefiting children. Various project-based action plans like National Child Labor Projects (NCLP) have been started in the areas of high concentration of child labor. As of now, there are 100 NCLPs in 13 child labor endemic states (see endnote 1).

Different *international agencies* like ILO, UNDP, UNICEF, UNDCP, UNFPA, UNIFEM, UNAIDS etc. have taken various initiatives to abolish and/or minimize the problem of child labor in India along with the rest of the world. ILO, the principal organization working on the problem of child labor, came up with many significant *Conventions* and *Recommendations* for ratification by the individual countries. Some of the important ILO Conventions ratified by India include Convention No. 5: Minimum Age (Industry) 1919, Convention No. 123: Minimum Age (Underground Work) 1965, Convention No. 6: Night Work for Young Persons (Industries) 1919, Convention No. 15: Minimum Age (Trimmers Stokers) 1921, and Convention No.16: Medical Examination of Young Persons (Sea) 1921. There are *eight core conventions* which ILO termed as fundamental/human rights conventions of which four conventions have been ratified by the Government of India but it did not ratify the other four for various reasons. The four ratified conventions are

i)   Forced Labor Convention (Convention No, 29)
ii)   Abolition of Forced Labor Convention (Convention No, 105)
iii)   Equal Remuneration Convention (Convention No, 100) and
iv)   Discrimination (Employment Occupation) Convention (Convention No, 111).

The four non-ratified conventions by the Indian government are

i)   Freedom of Association and Protection of Right to Organized Convention (No.87)
ii)   Right to Organize and Collective Bargaining Convention (No.98)
iii)   Minimum Age Convention (No.138) and
iv)   Worst forms of Child Labor Convention (No.182).

Child labor covered by the core ILO Convention No. 138 on Minimum Age and the Convention on the Elimination of the Worst Forms of Child Labor merit careful consideration. The latter convention commits countries to work with the ILO to fix time-bound policies to eliminate the worst forms of child labor. But the International Labor Standards and the Core Conventions of the ILO are still mired in a debate between the developed world led by the USA and the developing world led by the countries like China, India, and Brazil. The debate which started from the Uruguay Round of talk of WTO at Marrakech continued in Singapore, Doha, Seattle, and Cancun has become the core issue at the WTO negotiations where a lack of common ground has led to a virtual deadlock in negotiations. To the author this is an important debate where we can find conflict of interests and differences in perceptions regarding child labor between the West and the Third World. The Western world, oblivious about the problem of child labor in their own countries, failed to comprehend the ground realities in the Third World countries which lead to the proliferation of child labor. Thus the debates on the International Labor Standards and the Core Conventions of ILO have reached to such an enormous level that it is threatening a complete breakdown of WTO negotiations. *Other important international initiatives* include IPEC (International Program on the Elimination of Child Labor) by ILO, Program for Street Children by UNDCP, UNESCO's Learning Without Frontiers (LWF), activities on Child Trafficking by UNAIDS and Social Labeling of Child Labor Products by various agencies.

Almost all these initiatives did not produce any perceptible change in the ground realities on child labor in the Third World. For example, the most popular initiative in the West against the practice of child labor is "boycotting their product" that is applicable to products made by multinational companies like Nike, Reebok or Wal-Mart which have frequently being accused of using child labor to make their products cheaper. But this practice of boycotting has not solved the problem. On the contrary, it has created new problems as these multinational corporations decided to move the factories out of the country or simply cancel their demands in the face of an international hue and cry leaving the poor people in the Third World more vulnerable to starvation. Similar situation prevailed over the "social labeling" initiatives from the Western countries as the producers who had once employed child labor stopped this practice and started employing adult cheap laborers not necessarily from the families of the ousted child labor. This rendered those families more vulnerable and the children who were retrenched started working in some other sectors. Indeed, it is just like the opium, it makes you sicker and sicker, yet you cannot survive without it. At the same time, it does not mean that one must accept the fact that an unacceptable number of children who are at the dawn of the third millennium should still live without dignity. The biggest problem now is to get a proper roadmap to change the current child labor situation without damaging the economy of the Third World countries like India.

The Research Design

Formulating an appropriate research design for this work was a serious challenge for the author as an anthropologist particularly because the discipline of anthropology has been a late entrant in taking up issues like urban poverty, urban mar-

ginalization, ethnic tension in a city, urban communal violence, etc. and till recently anthropologists continued to focus on their traditional target groups i.e.
tribal and peasant people in urban settings. This trend started to change from the
late 1960s as various ethnographic studies on urban setting emerged during that
period. Thus Elliot Liebow's (1967) study on the marginalized people in urban
areas and more recently Philippe Bourgois's account of street culture in East
Harlem (1995) became trend-setters in the ethnographic studies in city.

The author studied the factors at the household level responsible for the creation and proliferation of child labor such as aspects related to the poverty and
vulnerability of the households like the incidences of unemployment in the family, types of primary occupation, level of daily income and monthly savings, parental perception on children, size of the families, child-woman ratio, literacy
rates and standard etc. Along with these factors the research design of this work
also included factors beyond the level of households responsible for child labor
like the conditions of urban marginality defined by collective consumption viz.
school, living condition of the household, security of tenure of the settlement.
Other factors in this category over which individuals and families had little control included the demand for child labor, the efficacy of legal and other initiatives to prevent child labor, cultural contexts of child labor and the forces of
globalization abetting the child labor problem in the Third World countries. This
research design strived to incorporate all these factors in the present study.

As briefly mentioned earlier, this research drew findings from three different
settlements referred to as Population - I, Population - II and Population – III in
the city of Kolkata in this study. These settlements located in the Ward Nos. 65
and 36 of Kolkata Municipal Corporation (KMC) respectively were studied intensively over a decade (i.e. from 1992 to 2002). Of the settlements studied here
Population - I and Population - II were squatter settlements, inhabitants lived
without any security of tenure as well as with almost no state provided or mediated basic services. Population - III, on the other hand, was a recognized slum
settlement in the Ward No. 59 of KMC where the inhabitants lived (and still
living) with some kind of security of tenure by virtue of an act [Calcutta *Thika*
and Other Tenancies and Lands (Acquisition and Regulation) Act, 1981]. The
author considered Population - I and Population - II collectively as the Control
Group and Population – III, where a program in the form of security of tenure
was employed from 1981 by virtue of the aforesaid act, as the Program Group.
Empirical findings in the form of quantitative results as well as thick description
of the key behaviors in the Control Group and the Program Group, suggested
that the groups differed substantially and the manifestation of the problem of
child labor varied between these two groups. With this outline, the author ga-
thered data on this problem which would enable a Third Worldly understanding
of this problem. The author also argued that being an anthropologist from the
Third World he was relatively better positioned to do that.

The next major task after the selection of sites was to *gain entry in the fieldsites.* In most cases, local contacts were used. The author carried his identity
documents all along the fieldwork period and allowed himself to be introduced

by the local contacts to the people in all the fieldsites. Some introductory state-
ments on the motive, use of the fieldwork for the population under study etc.
always proved to be very useful during this fieldwork. Even though the process
of initial contact went smoothly, the author frequently felt that the act of fieldwork was a fairly turbulent process. As Bernard (1988, pp. 164-165) puts it,
"some form of depression and shock thereafter (within a week or two). One kind
of shock comes as the novelty of the field site wears off and there is this nasty
feeling that anthropology has to get done .... Another kind of shock is to the
culture itself. Culture shock is an uncomfortable stress response, and must be
taken very seriously". During this fieldwork, the author was confronted with
those shocks and sometimes even had to take some temporary breaks in his
fieldwork to tide over the initial disorientation. At times *rapport building* in this
fieldwork proved to be very difficult as the nature of this research did not always
permit the author to spend much time with the informants for rapport building.
Hence, at many times, instead of asking for the 'meaning' of particular facts, he
questioned on the 'use' of those facts as the meaning emerged from repeated
observation or participant observation of the facts or events. The *selection of*
informants of informants was determined by the factors like enculturation of the
person concerned as the realities associated with the phenomenon of child labor
were quite unique. Thus factors like the informant's representativeness in the
population, articulating power, ability to follow the method of investigation and
the person who could act as intermediaries in this research played a key role in
the selection of informants. During this fieldwork open-ended semi-structured
interviewing with the informants was most useful in most of the situations. During the *selection a key informant* in this fieldwork, the author looked for some
additional factors in an individual like knowledge about the topic of interest,
involvement in the domain of interest or recently experienced, contemplative
nature, staying around in the population for a while and an ability to forge a social relationship with the author. Key informant interviewing techniques in this
fieldwork included iteration of the previous interview, providing probing stimuli,
posing leading questions, rephrasing incomprehensible questions, using informant responses and keeping provision of further meeting. In many cases the
author let the key informants to select the settings for interviewing and mostly
recorded these key interviews in written notes and in tape recorders. Informal
interviews, semi-structured interviews and standardized open-ended interviews
all were used in different phases during the key interviewing in this fieldwork.

The author had to compile some of his findings of this fieldwork as *non-*
participant observer i.e. by spending more time in the field setting to collect
observation data without significantly interacting with the subjects. Most of the
non-participant observations used during this fieldwork were unstructured focused observation especially during the initial exploratory part of this study and
structured observation as an effort to quantify the record of some of the key behaviors. On the other hand, there were many observations conducted during this
fieldwork that were participatory in nature whose salience had been enhanced by
staying with the informants and participating in their daily lives as far as possi-

ble. As is well known this form of unobtrusive-unstructured form of observation is considered as the *sine qua non* of any long-term ethnography. In this fieldwork, a good deal of time and rapport-building became necessary before informants stopped noticing the novelty of fieldworker's presence as a researcher and participation, and could go about their daily routine unaffected by his presence. Moreover, the author tried to attend the ethics of information gathering and possessing information about the daily activities of people who might come to think of the participant observer as more of a participant than an observer, with the attendant level of confidence that produces. *Participant observation* in this fieldwork mostly consisted of staying in the field for longer hours and following the scheme of 'speech-in-action'. According to this scheme a situational continuum is followed which usually ranges from the informant's turf – finding the informants where they are – and the ethnographer's turf and control (see Agar 1983). The author would like to mention here that the 'speech-in-action' followed (though not literally) particularly during the key informant interviewing, in most cases, ended in the shared control stage. The author was careful in this regard due to the specific nature of these fieldsites. Though the author did not actually stay with the people in the Control Group, he extended the hours of his fieldwork by reaching the site early in the morning and leaving late in the evening. The author actually stayed few nights with the Program Group population. He was always careful during this fieldwork not to disturb the daily routine of the participants.

Free lists and ranking were used during this fieldwork to determine and rank the socially cognizant items among the people under study. Case study was another frequently employed technique used in this fieldwork. Case study proved to be very useful during the advanced stages of the fieldwork when the relationship with informants grew considerably and the informant was on the researcher's turf with control share or the researcher in control. *Data analysis* in any anthropological research, including this work, usually takes place throughout the time-span of the research work as going back and forth with data refines the ideas on our research goals. The author also followed this tradition during this fieldwork. However, at the last stage of the research work, like other anthropologists, the author became fully involved with the analysis of the data collected from the fieldwork. In this fieldwork, the principal methods of data analysis consisted of repeated reading of fieldnotes, interview transcripts, site documents etc., marking the data, eliciting 'insiders' points of view, testing categories and explanations and triangulation among the various forms of data. With this research design the author tried to gather data from his field. The findings from this fieldwork suggest that we might need a paradigm shift as the existing theories, definitions and concepts on child labor cannot properly explain findings from this field.

The Findings

As indicated earlier, the author *selected three populations* on the basis of their different position of marginality in the city of Kolkata. The Population - I and the Population - II constituted the Control Group where the residents did not have any security of tenure i.e. people living in these settlements did not hold the title to their lands or their housing structures before they got evicted from the studied area. Population - III, on the other hand, represented the Program Group as a recognized slum or *bustee* settlement for more than two decades where the government subsequently authorized the settlers' right to live on the land under the Calcutta *Thika* and Other Tenancies and Land (Acquisition and Regulation) Act (1981). The author treated the data of all the three settlements separately and then combined the data of Population - I and Population - II and finally these combined data were compared with the data of Population - III.

a) Profile of the Populations

The *age and sex-wise* distribution (*Table – 1*) showed that the Control Group had more people in the age groups below 15 years than the other age groups (46.21 per cent), a tendency normally attributed to the high birth rate. At the same time, the presence of persons over the age of 45 years was remarkably low i.e. only 17.84 per cent of the total population. This declining proportion of the older people was an indicative of low life expectancy among the marginalized people in the Third World urban areas. The trend was particularly noticeable among the females where this declining trend was particularly visible in the age group over 40 indicating that the living condition was even worse for the females. Program Group, on the other hand, showed a contrasting feature of population profile when compared with the Control Group. In the Program Group, 25.50 per cent of the population was under 15 years of age – almost half that of the Control Group. It indicated a much lower birth rate among the people in the Program Group. Here the highest proportion of people was found between 20 to 29 years of age, an indication of a better living condition of a particular population. People above the age of 45 had also survived better in the Program Group which revealed an improved life expectancy for these people.

b) Educational Aspects of the Populations

The educational profile of the populations was an important indicator of the overall quality of the life of the two groups as higher educational attainments indicate that the population lived in a more secure environment, This study revealed that the *literacy rate* in the Control Group was only 44 per cent while in the Program Group it was much higher at nearly 79 per cent - an indicative of a much better educational position in the Program Group. Predictably, the *child literacy rate* in the Control Group was much lower at 47 per cent. The trend was even lower among the girls, which reflected the generally lower social status of women. The author made a detailed case study on this issue (Case Study No. 1) and found that Farah, a 10 years old girl from Population - I, discontinued her study due to various domestic and financial constraints.

> **Case Study No. 1 (Population - I):** 'My name is Farah, I am 10 years old…living in this settlement since my birth…I have two brothers… one is elder than me and the other is younger …I can sign my name in Urdu…I learned how to read Kalma (Arabic verses of Koran) …I went to a nearby Madrasa school for few months but my parents withdrew me from that school…Yes, my elder brother still reads in a school and my younger brother is too young to get admission in a school… Now I work as a scrap-picker and sometimes as a scrap-sorter…After returning from the work I help my mother in the household activities…'

In the Program Group, an exceptionally high child literacy rate of 95 per cent suggested that the children of this generation in the Program Group were getting better educational opportunities. This trend was reaffirmed by the case of Sikha Adhikary (Case Study No. 2), an 11 year old girl from Population – III, who was continuing her study in a nearby school.

> **Case Study No. 2 (Population - III):** 'I am Sikha Adhikary… 11 years old. I have lived in this settlement since my birth… I read in Class V in a nearby Bengali-medium school for girls. I have an elder brother who reads in a nearby boys' school in class VII…I along with my elder brother take private tuition in the morning and then go to school…After I return from the school I play with my friends…At the dusk I again prepare my lessons…. Our mother keeps a very strict eye on our study…'

c) Condition of Urban Marginality of the Studied People

Holding ration card of the public distribution system was one of the most important criteria of legitimacy for a settler in the city of Kolkata during this fieldwork as for the possession of a ration card resident needed a valid permanent address. Possession of this ration card also ensured access to various services like subsidized food grains and other essential commodities including kerosene oil – an essential source of energy for the marginalized people – for a dweller of the city. This study showed that in the Control Group almost none of the settlers had a ration card as they did not have any valid permanent address. The negligible few individuals who possessed the ration card in the Control Group gave false addresses. People in the Program Group, however, did not have this problem as their settlement had been legitimized by the local authority and most of them had their own ration cards. But more than half of the possible *voters* were registered as the actual voters in the Control Group which was quite a contrast to the trend of the possession of ration cards. In the Program Group, this picture was much improved as the residents here did not have any obstacle to become legitimate voters. It would be interesting to note that despite being the legitimate voters the residents of the Control Group failed to obtain the status of the legitimate settlers in the city of Kolkata as they did not possess the all-important ration card of public distribution system and a legitimate permanent address. The author studied the case of Momena Begum in Population - I (Case Study No. 3) who in spite of being a bona fide voter did not get the status of a legitimate citizen of the city and was eventually evicted during this study period.

Case Study No. 3 (Population - I): 'My name is Momena Begum...aged 35 years. I am living in this settlement for the last twenty years... We (i.e. Momena and her husband) have names in the voters' list ...A local political leader has registered our names after we settled here...No, we do not have any ration card...We buy rice and kerosene from the (open) market with much higher price...But we have names in the voters' list for the last twenty years...They promised us to protect during the time of crisis...We always cast our votes according to the wish of the local leaders...Now when the information of the demolition of our settlement came to us, we went to those leaders... But they are saying that it is inevitable...The road has to be widened... We went to our local councilor...The councilor also repeated the same...Where shall we go after that (eviction) we just don't know...We left our home in Bangladesh long ago...we do not have a home here.....'

The author also studied the case of Santosh Manna in the Population III (Case Study No. 4) who was both a legitimate voter and had also obtained the right to live in the city by virtue of the aforementioned *Thika* Tenancy Act.

Case Study No. 4 (Population - III): 'I am Santosh Manna; my age is 42 years ... I have been living in this settlement for the last twenty five years... Originally I am from Medinipore (an adjoining district of the city of Kolkata)...When I settled here I applied for my family's ration cards through some locally influential people and I got those ration cards...It came as a great help for me during the time of crisis...At one point of time the ration card was the only recognized document for identification at the various stages of our life....I admitted my son in the school, applied for different subsidized services, registered my son's name in the employment exchange with the help those ration cards.. After I received the ration cards I could register my name in the electoral roll during early 1980s...Now they have given a photo-identity card (voter's identity card)... it is a very helpful gesture on behalf of the government...'

Some *collective consumption indicators* (*Table – 2*) were used for the households in all the three settlements to measure the extent of urban marginalization present in all three populations. All the households in the Control Group and the Program Group enjoyed the facility of an accessible primary school within 1 km of their households. But people in the Control Group lacked such facilities like an accessible hospital/health centre within 1 km, a *pucca* arterial road within the settlement, an effective garbage disposal system, a planned drainage system, a legally obtainable electricity, separate bathrooms for families and its own tap as a source of drinking water. These facilities were more or less present in the Program Group and most of these facilities were available to all the residents of this settlement. Water logging during the rainy season was a common feature in all these three settlements. Most of the households in Control Group did not have completely water impermeable roofs, walls and floors whereas in the Program Group almost all the houses had water impermeable roofs, walls and floors. Separate ventilations and kitchens were present in a majority of the houses in the Program Group but only a few households in the Control Group could make such arrangements. Thus measurements of the indicators of urban marginality showed that the households in the Program Group were far better off in terms of the availability of these urban amenities (or collective consumption) facilities than the households in the Control Group. These findings would be particularly important in this analysis as almost all the child laborers studied during this fieldwork were from the Control Group which was definitely much more marginalized in terms of urban living.

d) Economic Condition of the Studied People

In the Control Group, it was found that both the *persons in labor force or labor force participation rate* (90 per cent participation rate) and the incidence of *persons actually working* (88 per cent participation rate) were very high. Female participation rate in the Control Group was also very high i.e. 85 per cent participation rate and nearly 81 per cent of the females were actually working. Contrary to popular belief that higher labor force participation rate indicate better economic participation, this trend actually indicated that the non-participation in work could result in starvation for these people who lived virtually at the subsistence level of the economy. In the Program Group, on the other hand, the incidences of labor participation were much lower with nearly 54 per cent rate of labor force in the population and 49 per cent was actually working. Female participation trends in labor force from the Program Group were even lower as only 25 per cent of these females were in labor force and only 22 per cent of them were actually working. These trends indicate the relative affluence of the residents of Program Group.

The *incidences of unemployment* showed that less than 3 per cent of the labor force in the Control Group was actually unemployed during the fieldwork. But most of the so-called employed people were actually engaged in some kind of unstable and subsistence level of work in the informal economy – a trend which can also be termed as incidences of 'misemployment'. In the Program Group, less than 9 per cent of the total persons in labor force were unemployed and the argument of misemployment can also be extended here as a substantial number of people in this group fell into the (mis)employment category. The distribution of the *children in labor force and children actually working (Table – 3)* revealed that in the Control Group nearly 90 per cent of the children were in the labor force and of them 84 per cent were actually working. Among these working children, boys and girls were in almost equal proportions. In the Program Group, on the other hand, less than 6 per cent were in labor force and a majority of them were actually working. Thus the distribution of the *working children compared with the working adults (Table – 4)* revealed that nearly 40 per cent of the work force in the Control Group were child laborers. In the Program Group this percentage was a mere two and half. It is the author's contention that a correlation could be drawn between the prevalence of child labor and urban marginality in the Third World which should pave the way for a new understanding of child labor in the Third World. During his review of relevant literature the author did not come across any references, by the Western and/or non-Western observers, where the phenomenon of child labor in urban areas has actually been taken up in relation to issues of urban marginalization particularly in terms of the security of tenure.

e) Findings on Child Labor: Population Profile

At the very onset of this section, it must be mentioned that since almost all the child laborers were from the Control Group, the data on child labor in the Control Group were almost identical with the overall trends on child labor in All Populations and the trends on child labor in the Program Group (which were different in many aspects) could not make any significant contribution on the overall trends on child labor in almost all the cases. Observations on the *age and sex wise distribution of the child laborers* (*Table – 5*) showed that more than half of the child laborers came from the age group of 10-14 years and rest were from the age group of 5-9 years. The frequency of boys was slightly higher than that of the girls among the working children. In the Program Group, on the other hand, the frequency of child laborers was negligible i.e. less than one per cent of the total population. In addition, all the child laborers from the Program Group were from the 10-14 years age group and the proportion of male child laborers (57 per cent) was higher than that of female child laborers. The author also observed the *age and sex- wise distribution of child laborers in comparison to the children in similar age group* (*Table – 6*) and was confronted with a grim reality as more than three fourth of the children in 5-9 years age group and more than 90 per cent of the children in 10-14 years age group were child laborers. It was further observed that nearly 80 per cent of the boys as well as more than 75 per cent of the girls in 5-9 years age group were working during this fieldwork. It was also observed during this fieldwork that more than 90 per cent of the boys as well as girls in 10-14 years age group were child laborers. In the Program Group, none of the children in the 5-9 years age group and only 9 per cent children in the 10-14 years age group were working. It was also observed that nearly eight and half per cent boys and ten per cent girls in the age group 10-14 years were child laborers in the Program Group.

f) Findings on Child Labor: Educational Profile

Study on the *educational standard* of these child laborers revealed that only 10 per cent child laborers had spent more than three years in school and nearly 30 per cent had between one to three years of schooling. In the Program Group, nearly 43 per cent child laborers had spent more than three years of schooling and rest had spent between one to three years in school. Findings on different aspects of education among these child laborers showed that as high as 54.48 per cent of the child laborers in All Populations had already dropped out of school. This trend was particularly visible among the child laborers in the Control Group where 54.78 per cent of the child laborers were dropouts while 42.86 per cent (numbering only three) in the Program Group were had dropped out. This high dropout rate was consistent with state national trends (see endnote 2). It was also observed from this distribution that only 7.53 per cent of these child laborers were continuing their study in formal schools during the time of this fieldwork. This trend was even lower in the Control Group (6.25 per cent) but much higher in the Program Group (57.14 per cent). On the other hand, majority (37.99 per cent) of the child laborers who were continuing their study during the fieldwork and reading in the non-formal schools run by some NGOs. This trend of reading in non-formal schools was found only in the Control Group.

The main reason that these children *left or were not sent to school* varied from the families' need of the children's contribution (nearly 40 per cent) to the inability of the families to afford schooling (nearly 38 per cent). In 20 per cent cases the children needed money to meet their own needs as the family could not support them. Other such reasons included children's lack of interest in studies (5 per cent) and a greater keenness in learning a practical skill as an apprentice to a skilled worker which accounted for nearly 4 per cent of the child laborer population. In the Control Group this trend was almost identical where the most frequent responses were the families' inability to continue the study (38 per cent) or the families' need for the children's contribution (nearly 35 per cent). This trend was not so much visible in the Program Group where in most of the cases the main reason for leaving school was the shift of interest to the apprenticeship to a skilled job (nearly 67 per cent). But again this trend in the Program Group could hardly alter the overall trend in this regard among the child laborers.

Thus the population and educational profiles of the child laborers indicate that almost all of the child laborers were from the Control Group where most of the children (except from the age group of 0-5 years of age) were child laborers. Most of these child laborers were either deprived of school education or had somehow managed to cling on the non-formal school, albeit irregularly. This trend can give an idea on condition of child laborers especially in the Control Group. Program Group, on the other hand, had managed to remain almost free from the problem of child labor though they started from dire economic conditions when they started living in that settlement. Thus it can again be argued that the security of tenure along with other factors played crucial role in the remarkable development of the Program Group.

g) Findings on Child Labor: Economic Profile

As the population and educational profile of the child labor indicated that the child laborers were eking out subsistence for themselves and their families in various ways. This reality would be further underline if we study the economic profile of the child labor population understudy.

The author observed the distribution of the *child laborer population according to the status as a laborer* (*Table – 7*). It showed that the overwhelming proportions of the child laborers in All Populations were wage earners (80.65 per cent) followed by the household businesses/occupations (11.30 per cent) or self-employed (8.05 per cent). The trend in the Control Group was quite similar as

81.22 per cent child laborers were wage-earning child laborers, 10.80 per cent were involved in the household businesses/occupations and 7.98 per cent were self employed. In the Program Group, however, most of the child laborers were in the household businesses/occupations (57.14 per cent). The girls were more frequently employed in the household businesses/occupations (7.59 per cent) than their male counterpart (3.72 per cent). Thus the girls, apart from in their own household occupations/businesses, were more likely to be employed in the other occupations which were household-based like domestic helps.

Observations on the *age of entering work* showed that most of the child laborers in All Populations entered work between the age of 6 years and 9 years (41 per cent) or between the age of 10 years and 14 years (39 per cent). A large section of these child laborers entered work at the tender age of below 6 years (nearly 20 per cent). This trend was even more visible among the girls (nearly 20 per cent) compared to the boys (8.50 per cent). This trend of large absorption of children in the workforce particularly in the Control Group during their school days was also substantiated by the very high frequency of non-literates among these children especially among the girls. Similar trends were also visible among the child laborers in the Control Group where more than 40 per cent entered in work between the ages of 6 years and 9 years, nearly 39 per cent between 10 years and 14 years and another 20 per cent entered below the age of 6 years. However, in the Program Group no child entered the workforce at the age of below 6 years and most of them entered between the ages of 10 years and 14 years.

Working hours of these child laborers were in most cases over 6 hours per day (nearly 75 per cent). In few cases these working hours ranged between 2 hours to 6 hours (14 per cent) or less than 2 hours (11per cent). A similar trend was also visible among the child laborers in Control Group where nearly 75 per cent worked above 6 hours per day, 13 per cent worked for 2 hours to 6 hours per day and 11per cent worked for less than 2 hours per day. In the Program Group, only one boy worked above 6 hours per day while most of the child laborers here generally worked between 2 hours and 6 hours (71 per cent). But again this improved trend in the Program Group could not significant alter the overall trend of long working hours among the child laborers.

These working children were allowed to have very little *resting time within the working hours* as 60 per cent of the child laborers in All Populations got a rest of less than 30 minutes within their working hours. But a more noticeable fact was that as many as 36 per cent of these children did not get any rest during their working hours. There were, however, some child laborers who were allowed to rest for 30 minutes to one hour (less than 3 per cent). But none of them got a resting time of more than an hour. In the Control Group, the above trend was almost identical as 61 per cent of the child laborers got less than 30 minutes of rest and 37 per cent of them worked without any break within their working hours. However, in the Program Group most of the child laborers (nearly 85 per cent) allowed a resting time of 30 minutes to one hour.

The distribution of the *child laborers according to the number of working days in a week* also revealed that most of the child laborers in All Populations worked for 6 days a week (59.60 per cent) and a very high proportion of them worked on all the 7 days in a week (32.30 per cent). Other categories like working for 5 days (2.79 per cent), 4 days (2.01 per cent), 3 days (1.39 per cent) or less than 3 days in a week (2.01 per cent) occurred in much lesser frequencies. Similar trend was visible among the child laborers of in the Control Group where 59.62 per cent child laborers worked for 6 days a week and 32.08 per cent working on all the 7 days in a week. In the Program Group, this trend was also visible where 42.86 per cent worked on all the 7 days in a week and 57.14 per cent worked for 6 days a week. But it must be mentioned here that in the Program Group all the child laborers (one boy and two girls precisely) worked on all the 7 days in a week and in their domestic units where they ordinarily work under much less strains.

It was also revealed from this study that as many as 98 per cent of the child laborer in All Populations worked in the informal sector of economy. Only a few child laborers (1 per cent) were absorbed in the formal sector of the economy. They worked without any formal appointment and mostly did odd jobs in those establishments. In the Control Group, 99 per cent of the child laborers were employed in the informal sector while in the Program Group the proportion of child laborers in the informal sector was little lower (85 per cent) and correspondingly the proportion of child laborers in the formal sector was higher (15 per cent).

Distribution of the *child laborers according to the type of occupation* (see *Table – 8*) showed that most of these child laborers in All Populations were either engaged as urban waste recycle workers i.e. the Type – E occupation (42.72 per cent) or in different occupations as 'sellers of their labor to people for the personal service and consumption of the buyers instead of using their labor power to obtain a surplus value' i.e. the Type – C occupations (42.57 per cent). Some of these children were also engaged as apprentices to the skilled workers or handicraft persons or small merchants i.e. the Type – B (13.47 per cent) and few were in the 'traditional' or formal sector of economy i.e. Type – A (1.08 per cent), though as temporary workers, as well as in the occupations which the author called skin sellers exchanging their survival against the possibility of potential destruction or deterioration i.e. the Type – D occupations (0.31 per cent). A gender-wise frequency distribution showed (Type – E and Type – B occupations) male child laborers were more frequently engaged. On the other hand, female child laborers were more frequently employed in the Type – C occupations. In the Control Group, the trend relating to the type of primary occupation remained similar to the overall trend with 43.19 per cent of the child laborers in the Type – E occupations, 42.57 per cent in the Type – C occupations, 13.15 per cent in the Type – B occupations, 0.94 per cent in the Type – A occupations and 0.31 per cent in the Type – D occupations. A gender-wise distribution revealed almost identical features among the child laborers in All Populations. On the other hand, the trends in the Program Group were quite different where 42.86 per cent child laborers were engaged in the Type – B occupations, 42.86 per cent in the Type – C occupations and 14.29 per cent in the Type – A occupations. None of these child laborers in the Program Group were engaged in the Type – D and the Type – E occupations. No female child laborer in the Program Group was found in the Type – A occupations and lesser proportion of female child laborers were found in the Type – B occupations while the proportion of female child laborers in the Type – C occupations were greater than in Type - B.

The distribution of the *details of the individual occupations* (see *Table – 9*) was also studied by the author and it corroborated the earlier findings on primary occupations. Most frequently found occupational type among the child laborers was the Type – E occupations. He found that the frequency of scrap pickers (30.34 per cent) was much higher than the other occupations in this type like scrap sorters (7.28 per cent) and door-to-door scrap buyers (5.11 per cent). Male child laborers were engaged more frequently in the Type – E occupations i.e. as scrap pickers (14.86 per cent), door to door scrap buyers (4.18 per cent) or scrap sorters (4.02 per cent). The next most frequent category of occupations among these child laborers was the Type – C occupations where as many as 21.21 per cent children were engaged as domestic helps (all of them were girls) and 7.12 per cent were tea stall/restaurant workers (majority of them were boys). Rest of the child laborers in this category were working as the helpers in construction works (2.94 per cent), porters (2.63 per cent), van/rickshaw pullers (2.32 per cent), *bidi* (flavored Indian cigarette wrapped in *tendu* leaf) -workers (2.32 per cent), shoe-shiners (2.01 per cent), *thonga* (paper-packet) -makers (0.62 per cent) and miscellaneous other occupations not falling under the earlier types (1.39 per cent). All the child laborers who worked as porters and van/rickshaw pullers were males but among the helpers in the construction works boys and girls were in almost equal proportions. Boys dominated the frequency (1.39 per cent) in the category of *bidi*-workers whereas in the category of shoe-shiners girls were more frequent (1.08 per cent) while all the *thonga* making child laborers were girls. In the Type – B occupations most of the child laborers were apprentice to the skilled workers or handicraft persons (12.69 per cent) and boys were in overwhelming majority among these apprentices (more than 90 per cent of this category). A tiny proportion of the child laborers engaged in the Types – B occupations were small merchants like fruit sellers, candy sellers etc. (0.77 per cent) and all of them were boys. The child laborers in the Type – A occupations engaged as temporary workers without any formal contract (1.08 per cent) were all boys. In the Control Group, the author found a similar trend in the Type – E occupations with 30.67 per cent child laborers were working as scrap pickers, 7.36 per cent scrap sorters and 5.33 per cent door-to-door scrap buyers (5.33 per cent). In the Type – C occupations the author found 21.44 per cent child laborers working as domestic helps, 7.04 per cent as tea stall/restaurant workers, 2.97 per cent as helpers in construction works, 2.66 per cent as porters, 2.35 per cent as van/rickshaw pullers, 2.35 per cent as *bidi* -workers, 2.03 per cent as shoe shiners, 0.31 per cent as *thonga*-makers while 1.41 per cent were engaged in other occupations. Gender-wise distribution of the child laborers in these occupations also showed an almost identical tendency with the distribution of the child laborer in All Populations. In the Program Group, as indicated earlier, a rather different picture emerges as none of the child laborers was engaged in the Type – D and the Type – E occupations. In the Program Group child laborers were also engaged in the Type – C occupations. Of them 28.57 per cent were *thonga*-makers (all girls) and 14.29 per cent were tea stall/restaurant workers (the only child labor in this category was a boy). In the Type – B occupations 28.57 per cent child laborers (divided evenly between male and female) were apprentices to skilled workers/handicraft persons and only one of them (14.29 per cent) was a male small merchant. The Type – A occupation only consisted of one temporary worker in the traditional sector of economy (14.29 per cent).

This study also noted that as many as 23.37 per cent of the child laborers in All Populations were employed in the occupations, services and industries which were declared prohibited under the Child Labor (Prohibition and Regulation) Act, 1986 promulgated by the Government of India. This trend of employing children in the hazardous occupations, services and industries was only found in the Control Group where 23.63 per cent child laborers were in hazardous jobs. On the other hand, none of the child laborers in the Program Group was in hazardous occupations, services and industries.

Distribution of the *child laborers according to the level of daily income (Table – 10)* showed that the daily incomes of 38.70 per cent child laborers in All Populations were between INR 10/- (20 cents) and INR 25/- (50 cents) while 28.02 per cent child laborers earned less than INR 10/- (20 cents) in All Populations. As high as 25.85 per cent child laborers had daily earnings more than INR 25/- (50 cents) but less than INR 50/- ($ 1.00) in All Populations while 7.43 per cent child laborers in All Populations were earning more than INR 50/- ($ 1.00) per day which was considered as a good income level among these marginalized people. Among the child laborers in the Control Group this trend on the level of daily income was almost identical with 27.86 per cent child laborers earning less than Rs. 10/- (10 cents) per day. One striking feature noticed among child laborers in the Program Group was that as many as 42.86 per cent child laborers had daily income of less than INR 10/- (20 cents). An explanation can be drawn from the fact that all the child laborers (i.e. a boy and two girls) in the Program Group were employed in the low-income family enterprises and their contributions were very limited in those enterprises.

None of the workplaces of these child laborers had adequate *hazard prevention mechanisms*. In 9 per cent of the workplaces, hazard prevention mechanisms though present, were inadequate while as high as 14.86 per cent of the workplaces hazard prevention mechanisms were completely absent despite the hazardous nature of the work. For as high as 76.63 per cent of these child laborers the hazard prevention facilities were not actually required because of the less risky nature of their work. In the Control Group, this trend was almost identical with nearly 9 per cent child laborers did not have adequate hazard prevention facilities and another 15 per cent did not have any hazard prevention mechanism even though they worked in different hazardous industries. On the other hand, none of the child laborers in the Program Group did not need hazard prevention mechanisms as they did not work in hazardous industries. Among the child laborers in All Populations, 21.36 per cent workplaces did not have *self protection measures* even though it was required, while in only 2 per cent of these workplaces had self protection measures though inadequate. In 76.63 per cent cases these measures were not required as they were not working in hazardous conditions. In the Control Group this trend was almost identical as in none of the workplaces involving child labor the self protection measures were adequately present. In 21.60 per cent of the cases these measures were completely absent while in 2.03 per cent of the cases the self protection measures in place were inadequate. In the Program Group, as indicated above, none of the child laborers was working in hazardous conditions and thus did not need any self protection measure. As far as the presence of *first aid facilities* in the work places of the child laborers in All Populations was concerned, as high as 91 per cent workplaces did not have any such facilities. Though it must be mentioned here that in most of these cases child laborers were not working in hazardous conditions but the complete absence of any first aid facility in the workplaces where the children work could not be justified as one can get injured in the safest work environment. It was also seen that in nearly 9 per cent cases some first aid facilities were present while in none of these work places those facilities were adequate. In the Control Group this trend was almost similar with nearly 65 per cent of these child laborers being deprived of any first aid facility in their work places while 8 per cent had inadequate first aid facilities in their workplaces. In none of the workplaces these facilities were adequately present. None of the child laborers in All Populations had adequate *toilet facilities* at their workplaces. 35 per cent of the workplaces toilet facilities had inadequate toilet facilities while 65 per cent had none at all. Similarly, in the Control Group 65 per cent child laborers did not have any toilet facility in their workplaces while 35 per cent of the workplaces involving child laborers had inadequate facilities. None of the workplaces were with adequate toilet facility. In the Program Group, more than 70 per cent workplaces had inadequate toilet facilities and 28 per cent of the child laborers did not have access to any toilet facilities in their workplaces.

A study on the *number of accidents happened to the working children in their working life*, revealed that 44 per cent child laborers in All Populations experienced different types of accidents two to five times in their working life even when they had not been working in the hazardous jobs while 9.44 per cent of these child laborers faced accidents for more than five times in their working life and almost all of them had been working in hazardous conditions. However, the author could not find a single case where a permanent damage to any part of the body or organ happened among these child laborers due to these accidents. All child laborers who suffered accidents belonged to the Control Group. The author would like to stress here that none of these accidents actually happened among the child laborers in the Program Group.

The author also found that most of the child laborers in All Populations worked either in units with five to ten fellow employees (51 per cent) or in the units having less than five fellow employees (36 per cent). Only 12.00 per cent worked in the units having more than ten fellow employees. An almost identical trend was found in the Control Group where more than half of the wage earning child laborers worked in the units with five to ten fellow employees, while more than 36 per cent in the units with less than five fellow employees and 12 per cent in the units with more than ten fellow employees. In the Program Group, only two children were wage earners. One worked in a unit having less than five fellow employees while the other in a unit with five to ten fellow employees.

More than 40 per cent of the wage earning child laborers in All Populations received their own wages. In other cases the recipients included the parents, the father (in 20 per cent cases), then the mother (in 10 per cent cases), or other male members of the family (22 per cent). In 6 per cent of the cases relatives or neighbors received the wages of the working children. In the Control Group the trend was again almost identical with 40 per cent of the wage earning children received their own wages. The author found that the parents received wages for their children in 26 per cent cases and for 22 per cent wage earning children the wages were received by other elder member of the family while 6 per cent cases the wages were received by other relatives or neighbors of the children. In the Program Group all the wage earning children received their own wages.

The study on the behavior of the *fellow adult employees in the workplace* showed that nearly 73 per cent of the wage-earning children in All Populations occasionally received harsh behavior from their fellow adult employees. But significant proportion (nearly 23 per cent) of them frequently met harsh behaviors from the fellow adult employees while very few of them (4 per cent) were not treated harshly by the fellow adult employees. In the Control Group, this trend was almost identical with 73 per cent of these wage earning children occasionally received harsh behaviors from their fellow adult employees and another 23.04 per cent frequently met harsh behaviors from their fellow adult employees. In the Program Group, on the other hand, all the wage earning children occasionally were occasionally treated with harsh behavior from their fellow adult employees.

The *behavior of the employers with the child laborers* also varied as 73 per cent of the child laborers in All Populations occasionally received harsh behaviors from their employers and a significant proportion of them (nearly 23 per cent) frequently experienced harsh behavior from their employers. Only 4 per cent of these wage earning children did not experience harsh behavior from their employers. In the Control Group this trend was almost similar as nearly 73 per cent of the wage earning children occasionally met harsh behavior and another 23 per cent frequently met harsh behaviors from their employers while only 4 per cent of these child laborers were never treated harshly by their employers. In the Program Group, on the other hand, all the wage earning children occasionally met harsh behaviors from their employers.

The *mode of receiving wage or income* of these child laborers in All Populations showed that more than half of the received weekly wages or incomes whereas nearly 26 per cent received daily wages or incomes and only a few (7 per cent) received monthly wages or incomes. Since more than 10 per cent child laborers were engaged in family businesses or enterprises they did not receive any income or wage. In the Control Group one can find an almost identical trend of the mode of receiving wage or income with 54 per cent child laborers received weekly wages/incomes, 27 per cent daily wages/incomes and 7 per cent monthly wages/incomes. In the Program Group, on the other hand, 57 per cent child laborers were engaged in family enterprises or businesses and did not receive any wage/income while 43 per cent received weekly wages/incomes.

There is a popular perception that the child laborers do not have family or family support, which may be true for some other Third World cities. But in Kolkata this belief proved to be completely wrong as all the child laborers in both the Control Group and the Program Group had their own families. The author also found that more than 65 per cent of these child laborers contributed more than fifty per cent of their earnings and nearly 19 per cent between ten to fifty per cent of their earnings to their household budgets. Some of them (nearly 11per cent) contributed less than ten per cent of their earnings to their households and even fewer (nearly 5 per cent) contributed nothing to their households. In the Control Group, the trend was almost similar with 65 per cent of the child laborers contributed more than fifty per cent of the earnings, 18 per cent between ten to fifty per cent of the earnings, 11 per cent less than ten per cent of the earning while 5 per cent contributed nothing to their households. In the Program Group, more than 85 per cent of child laborers contributed their entire earnings to their families and 15 per cent of them contributed ten to fifty per cent of their earnings to their families.

A study on the *level of dependence of the household* on the income of child labor showed that for 71 per cent families of the child laborers in All Populations the dependences was substantial. Nearly 25 per cent families were nominally dependent and less than 5 per cent families were not dependent on the earnings of their children. On the other hand, less than 1 per cent of families of these child laborers were entirely dependent on income of their working children. In the Control Group, similar trend of dependence was found where more than 71 per cent of the families of child laborers were substantially dependent on their incomes, 23 per cent nominally dependent, 5 per cent not dependent and less than 1 per cent was completely dependent on their incomes. In the Program Group, these families were either substantially dependent (57.14 per cent) or nominally dependent (42.86 per cent) on their working children's incomes.

The author also found that 44 per cent of the child laborers in All Populations had never left their job while nearly 35 per cent of them had left just once. Nearly 15 per cent of them, however, had left their jobs two to five times and nearly 7 per cent left more than five times. A similar trend was observed in the Control Group with nearly 45 per cent of the child laborers had never left their jobs and 35 per cent left just once while 15 per cent left two to five times and 42 per cent had left their jobs for more than five times. In the Program Group, on the contrary, nearly 58 per cent of the child laborers had never left their jobs and nearly 29 per cent had left just for once.

A study on the *reasons for quitting jobs* among these child laborers showed that nearly 15 per cent child laborers in All Populations quit their jobs owing to the intolerable working condition, 14 per cent because the pay was too low and nearly 12 per cent due to the accident-proneness of the job. Other reasons included getting fired or being terminated for 8 per cent child laborers, leaving to learn a skilled and more lucrative job (3 per cent), having to travel too far to go to the work place (2 per cent) or for some other reasons like abuse, boredom of the work etc. (1 per cent). In the Control Group, similar trend was found where 15 per cent child laborers left the job due to intolerable working conditions, nearly 13 per cent for very low pay, nearly 11 per cent for the accident proneness of the job, 8 per cent fired or terminated, 3 per cent because they wanted to learn a skilled and more lucrative job, 2 per cent because they had to travel too far distance to reach to their work places and 1per cent due to some other reasons. In the Program Group, on the other hand, all the child laborers who left their jobs attributed their decision to very low pay.

The author also undertook some qualitative studies on their key behaviors. Foremost among those studies was the attitude of the parents toward the children in these two groups. In the Control Group, the author frequently found regular examples of maltreatments to the children. During this fieldwork, the author was witness to incidents like beating the children by their parents on trivial issues, children playing in dirty conditions without the attention of their parents and defecating on the open space on the insistence of their parents. The author also found that the boys were given preferential treatment over the girls and earning children were preferred over the non-working children in the same family etc. All these indicated that the children (particularly the girl children) were not viewed favorably by the parents in the Control Group as a potential resource for their future. Thus they were not prepared to make an investment for the education of their children as these investments could not bring any immediate improvement in the quality of life of their children as well as their families. In the Program Group, on the other hand, the children were much better looked after as the education was considered as an important component of the life of these children. All the children in the Program Group were sent to school. The author found that the parents could afford the education of their children and they considered their children as their future resources who could look after their parents later during their old age. There were fewer incidents of abusing children by their parents in the Program Group. It must be mentioned here that in the Program Group also the boys were preferred over the girls which is almost a universal feature throughout South Asia. In the Program Group very few children were actually working. The author could find only three working children from this group and in most cases their work was limited to extending a helping hand to their parents in their domestic unit of production or in domestic chores.

A study on the child laborers' own perceptions on their reality and future were also taken up in a limited way during this work. The author found that most of the working children could not think beyond the next day and they had accepted their reality as their destiny. They believed that their life was much harsher when they were not working as they were on the brink of starvation. Their vision of a better future was to become a skilled worker and earning better wages for themselves as well as for their families as they were not been able to think beyond the next day and could only perceive their future in terms of better earnings right from their childhood.

Thus a remarkably contrasting picture related to child labor was found among these two groups of populations, i.e. the Control Group and the Program Group. The study showed that a correlation could be drawn between the security of tenure and the problem of child labor in the Third World. The author found that in the Program Group the child labor had been almost entirely eradicated but this problem persisted in the Control Group as the author found that most children in the Control Group were involved with some form of work. The author also found various other factors like the income stability of the parents, level of family income etc. had determining effects on the problem of child labor in the Control Group. Thus he argued that the proliferation of child labor was inextricably bound with the security of their parents both in terms of housing as well as income, leading to a vicious cycle of exploitation and marginalization in a Third World country like India. The author has also argued that a change in the paradigm is required to properly comprehend the problem of child labor which would be able to incorporate various new insights on this predominantly Third World problem.

CHAPTER 4

TABLES

TABLE – 1   DISTRIBUTION OF THE POPULATIONS ACCORDING TO AGE AND SEX (PERCENTAGES)

AGE GROUP	POPULATION I			POPULATION II			POPULATION I & II			POPULATION III			ALL POPULATIONS		
	M	F	T	M	F	T	M	F	T	M	F	T	M	F	T
0 – 4	9.76	9.46	19.22	12.13	6.44	18.57	11.34	7.47	18.81	3.86	2.62	6.48	9.50	6.28	15.78
5 – 9	11.76	10.96	22.72	7.86	7.73	15.59	9.18	8.82	18.00	4.27	4.27	8.54	7.97	7.70	15.67
10 – 14	14.30	12.16	26.46	5.56	5.35	10.91	8.50	7.65	16.15	6.48	4.00	10.48	8.01	6.75	14.76
15 – 19	3.47	3.74	7.21	2.85	3.05	5.90	3.06	3.28	6.34	4.55	4.27	8.82	3.43	3.53	6.96
20 – 24	3.34	3.34	6.68	1.28	4.48	5.76	1.98	4.36	6.34	4.69	7.31	12.00	2.65	5.09	7.74
25 – 29	2.94	3.61	6.55	3.05	4.68	7.73	3.01	4.32	7.33	6.07	6.07	12.14	3.77	4.75	8.52
30 – 34	2.00	1.74	3.74	2.71	4.47	7.18	2.47	3.55	6.02	3.86	4.69	8.55	2.82	3.83	6.65
35 – 39	1.74	1.47	3.21	4.48	5.97	10.45	3.69	4.01	7.70	5.10	3.45	8.55	4.04	3.87	7.91
40 – 44	1.20	0.40	1.60	3.59	3.25	6.84	2.80	2.29	5.09	4.27	2.62	6.89	3.16	2.37	5.53
45 – 49	0.93	0.27	1.20	2.78	0.95	3.73	2.17	0.72	2.89	1.79	2.48	4.27	2.07	1.15	3.22
50 - 54	0.40	0.13	0.53	2.44	0.61	3.05	1.75	0.45	2.20	2.62	1.79	4.41	1.97	0.78	2.75
55 - 59	0.27	0.13	0.40	1.36	0.41	1.77	0.98	0.31	1.29	1.51	1.24	2.75	2.49	1.55	4.04
60+	0.40	0.00	0.40	1.42	1.52	2.94	1.08	0.76	1.84	3.09	2.90	5.99	4.17	3.66	7.83
ALL	52.54	47.46	100.00	51.68	48.32	100.00	52.01	47.99	100.00	52.27	47.73	100.00	52.07	47.93	100.00
NO. OF PERSONS	748 (100.00)			1475 (100.00)			2223 (100.00)			725 (100.00)			2948 (100.00)		

TABLE-2: DISTRIBUTION OF THE HOUSEHOLDS ACCORDING TO THE PRESENCE OF SOME INDICATORS ON COLLECTIVE CONSUMPTION (PERCENTAGES)

INDICATORS ON COLLECTIVE CONSUMPTION	HOUSEHOLDS IN POP - I	HOUSEHOLDS IN POP - II	HOUSEHOLDS IN POP - I & II	HOUSEHOLDS IN POP - III	HOUSEHOLDS IN ALL POP
Accessible primary school within 1 km	100.00	100.00	100.00	100.00	100.00
Accessible hospital/health centre within 1 km	0.00	0.00	0.00	100.00	28.00
Accessible playground within 1 km	0.00	0.00	0.00	100.00	28.00
Accessible community-centre within 1 km	0.00	0.00	0.00	100.00	28.00
Motorable road	100.00	100.00	100.00	100.00	100.00
Pucca arterial road within settlement	0.00	0.00	0.00	100.00	28.00
Garbage disposal system	0.00	0.00	0.00	100.00	28.00
Planned drainage system	0.00	0.00	0.00	100.00	28.00
Legally obtained electricity	0.00	0.00	0.00	98.09	30.13
Separate ventilation	1.12	5.26	3.89	85.71	26.80
Separate family bathroom	0.00	0.00	0.00	29.05	8.13
Separate kitchen	1.12	3.32	2.59	64.76	20.00
Water impermeable roof	31.29	34.90	33.70	60.48	41.20
Water impermeable wall	41.34	44.05	43.15	93.33	57.20
Water logging of floor during rainy season	66.48	67.87	64.41	3.33	49.47
Own household tap as a source of drinking water	0.00	0.00	0.00	10.00	2.80
No. of Households	179 (100.00)	361 (100.00)	540 (100.00)	210 (100.00)	750 (100.00)

TABLE - 3: DISTRIBUTION OF THE POPULATIONS ACCORDING TO THE CHILDREN IN LABOR FORCE AND THE CHILDREN ACUTALLY WORKING (PERCENTAGES)

CHILDREN IN LABOR FORCE AND ACTUALLY WORKING	POPULATION – I & II			POPULATION - III			ALL POPULATIONS		
	M	F	T	M	F	T	M	F	T
Children in Labor Force	90.59	89.07	89.86	6.41	5.00	5.80	40.24	36.68	76.92
Children in Actual Work	86.01	82.24	84.19	5.13	5.00	5.07	38.13	33.89	72.02
Total	100.00	100.00	100.00	100.00	100.00	100.00	100.00	100.00	100.00
No. of Children	393	366	759	78	60	138	471	426	897

TABLE - 4: DISTRIBUTION OF THE WORKING POPULATION ACCORDING TO THE WORKING CHILDREN AND THE WORKING ADULTS (PERCENTAGES)

WORIKING POPULATION	POPULATION – I & II			POPULATION - III			ALL POPULATIONS		
	M	F	T	M	F	T	M	F	T
Working Children	41.07	40.73	40.91	1.91	4.76	2.57	18.65	16.58	35.23
Working Adults	58.93	59.27	59.09	98.09	95.24	97.43	37.62	27.15	64.77
All Working Population	100.00	100.00	100.00	100.00	100.00	100.00	100.00	100.00	100.00
No. of Working People	823	739	1562	209	63	272	1032	802	1834

TABLE – 5: DISTRIBUTION OF THE CHILD LABORERS ACCORDING TO AGE AND SEX (PERCENTAGES)

AGE GROUP	CHILD LABORER IN POPULATION - I			CHILD LABORER IN POPULATION - II			CHILD LABORER IN POPULATION – I & II			CHILD LABORER IN POPULATION - III			CHILD LABORER IN ALL POPULATIONS		
	M	F	T	M	F	T	M	F	T	M	F	T	M	F	T
5 – 9 YEARS	23.62	20.06	43.69	27.58	26.36	53.94	25.67	23.32	48.98	0.00	0.00	0.00	25.39	23.07	48.46
10 – 14 YEARS	30.74	25.57	56.31	23.94	22.12	46.06	27.23	23.79	51.02	57.14	42.86	100.00	27.55	23.99	50.64
ALL	54.37	45.93	100.00	51.52	48.48	100.00	52.90	47.10	100.00	57.14	42.86	100.00	52.94	47.06	100.00
NO. OF CHILD LABORER	168	141	309	170	160	330	338	301	639	4	3	7	342	304	646

TABLE - 6: DISTRIBUTION OF THE CHILD LABORERS AND THE CHILDREN POPULATIONS ACCORDING TO AGE AND SEX (PERCENTAGES)

AGE GROUP	POPULATION - I			POPULATION - II			POPULATION – I & II			POPULATION - III			ALL POPULATIONS		
	M	F	T	M	F	T	M	F	T	M	F	T	M	F	T
CHILD LABORERS (5 - 9 YEARS)	82.95	75.61	79.41	78.45	76.32	77.39	80.39	76.02	78.25	0.00	0.00	0.00	25.39	23.06	48.45
CHILD LABORERS (10 – 14 YEARS)	88.79	86.81	87.88	96.34	92.41	94.41	92.06	89.41	90.81	8.51	10.34	9.21	27.55	23.99	51.54

TABLE – 7: DISTRIBUTION OF CHILD LABORERS ACCORDING TO THE STATUS AS A LABORER (PERCENTAGES)

TYPE OF WORK	CHILD LABORER IN POPULATION – I & II			CHILD LABORER IN POPULATION – III			CHILD LABORER IN ALL POPULATIONS		
	M	F	T	M	F	T	M	F	T
WAGE EARNING	45.13	36.31	81.22	28.57	0.00	42.86	44.74	35.91	80.65
SELF EMPLOYED	4.28	3.60	7.98	14.29	0.00	14.29	4.49	3.56	8.05
HOUSEHOLD BUSINESS/ OCCUPATION	3.60	7.20	10.80	14.29	42.86	57.14	3.72	7.59	11.30
ALL	52.90	47.10	100.00	57.14	42.86	100.00	52.94	47.06	100.00
NO OF CHILD LABORER	338	301	639	4	3	7	342	304	646

TABLE – 8: DISTRIBUTION OF CHILD LABORERS ACCORDING TO THE TYPE OF PRIMARY OCCUPATION (PERCENTAGES)

PRIMARY OCCUPATION	CHILD LABORER IN POPULATION – I & II			CHILD LABORER IN POPULATION – III			CHILD LABORER IN ALL POPULATIONS		
	M	F	T	M	F	T	M	F	T
(A)	0.94	0.00	0.94	14.29	0.00	14.29	1.08	0.00	1.08
(B)	12.21	0.94	13.15	28.57	14.29	42.86	12.38	1.08	13.46
(C)	15.65	26.91	42.56	14.29	28.57	42.86	15.63	26.94	42.57
(D)	0.31	0.00	0.31	0.00	0.00	0.00	0.00	0.31	0.31
(E)	23.79	19.25	43.04	0.00	0.00	0.00	23.53	19.04	42.57
ALL	52.90	47.10	100.00	57.14	42.86	100.00	52.94	47.06	100.00
NO. OF CHILD LABORER	338	301	639	4	3	7	342	304	646

A - SALARIED WORKERS OF 'TRADITIONAL' SECTOR OF THE ECONOMY

B - SKILLED WORKERS (*MISTRIS*), HANDICRAFT PERSONS AND SMALL MERCHANTS

C - SELLERS OF THEIR LABOR TO PEOPLE FOR THE PERSONAL SERVICE AND CONSUMPTION OF THE BUYERS INSTEAD OF USING THEIR LABOUR POWER TO OBTAIN A SURPLUS VALUE

D - SKIN SELLERS EXCHANGING THEIR SURVIVAL AGAINST THE POSSIBILITY OF POTENTIAL DESTRUCTION (e.g. PROSTITUTE*, DELINQUENT* etc.) OR TRADE THEIR DETERIORATION (e.g. BEGGAR)

E - URBAN WASTE RECYCLE WORKERS

TABLE – 9: DISTRIBUTION OF CHILD LABORERS ACCORDING TO THE PRIMARY OCCUPATION (DETAILS OF OCCUPATIONS) (PERCENTAGES)

	PRIMARY OCCUPATION	CHILD LABORER IN POPULATION – I & II			CHILD LABORER IN POPULATION – III			CHILD LABORER IN ALL POPULATIONS		
		M	F	T	M	F	T	M	F	T
A	TEMPORARY	0.94	0.00	0.94	14.29	0.00	14.29	1.08	0.00	1.08
	PERMANENT	0.00	0.00	0.00	0.00	0.00	0.00	0.00	0.00	0.00
B	APPRENTICE TO SKILLED WORKER, HANDICRAFT/PERSONS	11.58	0.94	12.52	14.29	14.29	28.58	11.61	1.08	12.69
	SMALL MERCHANT	0.63	0.00	0.63	14.29	0.00	14.29	0.77	0.00	0.77
C	DOMESTIC HELP	0.00	21.44	21.44	0.00	0.00	0.00	0.00	21.21	21.21
	PORTER	2.66	0.00	2.66	0.00	0.00	0.00	2.63	0.00	2.63
	VAN/RICKSHAW PULLER	2.35	0.00	2.35	0.00	0.00	0.00	2.32	0.00	2.32
	HELPER IN CONSTRUCTION	1.88	1.11	2.97	0.00	0.00	0.00	1.86	1.08	2.94
	TEA STALL/ RESTAURANT WORKER	5.16	1.88	7.04	14.29	0.00	14.29	5.26	1.86	7.12
	HELPER IN TRANSPORT	0.00	0.00	0.00	0.00	0.00	0.00	0.00	0.00	0.00
	SHOE- SHINER	0.93	1.10	2.03	0.00	0.00	0.00	0.93	1.08	2.01
	BIDI WORKER	1.41	0.94	2.35	0.00	0.00	0.00	1.39	0.93	2.32
	PACKET (*THONGA*) MAKING	0.00	0.31	0.31	0.00	28.58	28.58	0.00	0.62	0.62
	OTHER	1.25	0.16	1.41	0.00	0.00	0.00	1.24	0.15	1.39
D	BEGGAR	0.31	0.00	0.31	0.00	0.00	0.00	0.31	0.00	0.31
	PROSTITUTE	0.00	0.00	0.00	0.00	0.00	0.00	0.00	0.00	0.00
	DELINQUENT	0.00	0.00	0.00	0.00	0.00	0.00	0.00	0.00	0.00
E	SCRAP PICKER	15.49	15.02	30.51	0.00	0.00	0.00	15.30	14.86	30.19
	SCRAP BUYER (DOOR-TO-DOOR)	4.23	0.94	5.16	0.00	0.00	0.00	4.18	0.93	5.11
	SCRAP SORTER	4.07	3.29	7.36	0.00	0.00	0.00	4.02	3.25	7.27
	SCRAP DEALER	0.00	0.00	0.00	0.00	0.00	0.00	0.00	0.00	0.00
	ALL	52.90	47.10	100.00	57.14	42.86	100.00	52.94	47.06	100.00
	NO. OF CHILD LABORER	338	301	639	4	3	7	342	304	646

TABLE – 10: DISTRIBUTION OF CHILD LABORERS ACCORDING TO THE LEVEL OF DAILY INCOME (PERCENTAGES)

LEVEL OF DAILY INCOME*	CHILD LABORER IN POPULATION – I & II			CHILD LABORER IN POPULATION – III			CHILD LABORER IN ALL POPULATIONS		
	M	F	T	M	F	T	M	F	T
LESS THAN INR 10/-	11.58	16.28	27.86	14.29	28.57	42.86	11.61	16.41	28.02
INR 10/- TO 24/-	20.19	18.94	39.12	0.00	0.00	0.00	19.97	18.73	38.70
INR 25/- TO 49/-	16.90	8.76	25.67	28.57	14.29	42.86	17.03	8.82	25.85
INR 50/- OR MORE	4.23	3.13	7.36	14.29	0.00	14.29	4.33	3.09	7.43
ALL	52.90	47.10	100.00	57.14	42.86	100.00	52.94	47.06	100.00
NO. OF CHILD LABORER	338	301	639	4	3	7	342	304	646

CHAPTER 5

NEED FOR A PARADIGM SHIFT

Thus we have seen from this study that the existing interpretations on the problem of child labor cannot adequately explain the actual nature of the problem for various reasons. When the author started this study during the early 1990s little did he know that the outcome of this study would reflect the inadequacies of the existing body of knowledge on this issue. That was when India got onto the bandwagon of liberalization and globalization with rhetoric of providing "good life" to its citizens. But during this study, which spanned a decade, the author found that this journey did improve the quality lives of some people but proved to be a "race to bottom" for the overwhelming majority particularly in the Third World cities like Kolkata. Several individual studies and reports from the international agencies like UNCHS, UNDP, UNICEF, and WHO also indicated a similar bipolarization of the destiny of the people in the Third World in recent past. In the cities of Third World this trend is more pronounced as these cities became the primary destinations of capital and a rapid pace of its development left a huge proportion of people in these cities "excluded". This study has shown that this vast pool of "excluded" and marginalized population became the breeding ground for child labor in the Third World cities. There are various reasons associated with the creation of child labor among these marginalized people which have been discussed in this study. At the core all these explanations lies the fact that these people fail to perceive their children as their future force and they become less keen in the "deferred investment" for the education of their own children.

While dealing with the concepts of child labor for his present formulation the author found an urgent need for culturally relative concept(s) of child labor. This need is generated by the fact that almost all the definitions of child labor have either originated from the Western scholars or have derived from Western conceptual materials and have failed to explain the child labor situation in the Third World adequately. But the fact remains that a huge amount of fund are still getting mobilized by the international agencies like ILO, UNICEF, UNDP etc. to eradicate child labor in the Third World and almost all these allocations of fund are based on the basis of these Western or West-mediated concepts on the eradication of child labor. Thus, in spite of huge mobilization of funds to eradicate child labor in the Third World countries the problem has not only persisted but proliferated both in relative and absolute terms. The author argues that we are actually failing to address the basic issue that we need a new understanding – a paradigm shift – which can offer a Third World centric explanation of this problem. Even when such an analysis is attempted it also has the potential to create a range of controversies as any non-Western understanding of this problem can also be accused of bearing signs of a prior Western presence given that even the most amicable routes to decolonize anthropology might involve some sort of adversarial relationship with the West which immediately sets up a tension. This tension could be intensified as it calls for an erasing of colonial subjugation and equality claimed with the erstwhile masters. It is also the source of extreme anxiety for a non-Western anthropologist like the author himself because it seems to threaten any distinctive (non-Western) identity – which alone would be the proof of true equality. This anxiety would be multiplied by the current debates on the effect of globalization on non-Western societies. Thus an anthropologist's role in this morass has further been compounded by the fact that the discipline is still nursing its colonial wounds and till date most of the anthropological studies in non-Western societies have not been liberated from the thrall of Western knowledge both in terms of resources and intellectual influences. But developing culturally relative concepts of child labor is an important priority for an anthropologist.

So a shift has become imminent particularly in our study on this issue which would also include the voice(s) of the 'Other' (i.e. the child laborers and their families) to enable us to comprehend the actual nature of realities prevailing in different Third World situations. But to do this the discipline needs to develop a suitable research design which can incorporate the authentic self-expression of the actors (in this case the child laborers and their family members) of their reality. We need an appropriate research methodology which is inclusive in nature and which permits the Other to speak. Fieldwork techniques used in anthropology like the participant observation, the unstructured and semi-structured interviews and the like were tried during this research with an effort to make the study more inclusive. The author's own poverty-stricken childhood experience also helped to bring him closer to the reality of child laborers and their families in Kolkata. It also gave the author some additional understandings which proved to be methodologically important for an inclusive study as it became a kind of collaborative research. But the collaboration was somewhat impeded by the author's later acquired middle-class identity which came in between the world of these child laborers and the author. The need to translate from Bengali, the language in which the child laborers spoke to English, further undermined the project of inclusion. The author does not rule out translator's intervention in the self-expression of these child laborers on their reality as the narrations may not remain authentic after getting translated in a different language.

The readers already know that the author's work revolved around two groups of population viz. the Control Group and the Program Group. This division was based on the presence of a program of 'security of tenure' which the Program Group received for over a decade before the time of this study. The Control Group, however, was deprived of any security of tenure of the land on which they resided. During his long fieldwork the author observed various trends in these two groups and found some remarkable differences between them which revealed that the phenomenon of child labor was more complex than what it seemed from the available studies. Thus the study showed that the Control Group had more people under the age of 15 years indicating a higher birth rate compared to the Program Group. The literacy rate in the Control Group (44 per cent) was much lower than in the Program Group (79 per cent). The picture of child literacy was equally grim as only 47 per cent children in the Control Group were going to school compared to 95 per cent in the Program Group. This scenario indicated that the population living in the Control Group was less interested in the education of their children possibly due to the fact that most of the parents in this group were not literate and had stayed out of school during their childhood period. Many children in the Control Group were never sent to school which made them more prone to becoming child laborer at a very early age of their life. In the Control Group the author also found that apart from an apathy to send their children to school, the parents had a tendency to withdraw their children from their schools and send them out to work. The author's fieldwork also indicated that for various reasons parents as well as their children in the Control Group did not think education as an important prerequisite of their survival. One, they thought that the educational system could not equip them with the skills necessary to get meaningful job for them in foreseeable future. Two, the curricula were not motivating to the children and did not have any relation with the everyday realities they faced. Three, the families could not plan for the future since they had to eke out survival each day. And four, in addition to these day-to-day threats to their survival they had the specter of eviction constantly looming large on them which precluded the 'luxury' of investing in the education of their children which might bring results after few years. Sending their children to school also did not proved to be gainful for most of the parents in the Control Group as it prevented those children from working and supplementing the income for their families. The Program Group, on the other hand, did not have any of these impediments as most of the families had a more stable economic environment with more secured jobs and a far better living condition with no threats of eviction as they had a security of tenure of their houses which they were enjoying for decades.

The author also found that almost all people in the Control Group did not have any ration card of the public distribution system since they lacked the basic requirement of a legitimate permanent address. In contrast almost all the people in the Program Group had their own ration cards. These ration cards were the means for access to food grains and other essential commodities at subsidized rates. A ration card holder in the city of Kolkata also has access to various municipal services like water, electricity etc. The author found that though the adult men and women of the Control Group could exercise their rights to vote in the elections and they had names on the electoral roll, they were not regarded as the legitimate dwellers in the city of Kolkata as they did not possess any ration card. The author found it as a unique kind of deprivation as the right to have a vote did not guarantee these people in the Control Group the right to live in the same place and the lack of the right to possess a ration card due the absence of a legitimate address led to the breach of their rights to have equal access to subsidized food grains and other essential commodities which they needed most. This is only a Third World city like Kolkata that the right to vote, widely considered a fundamental right, is subordinate to the right to access subsidized food grains and other essential commodities. In other cities in the developed world those people who have the right to vote in a particular area also have the associate rights like right to live and right to have an equal access to the subsidized services available in that area.

The author also found that there were huge differences in the economic condition of the people living in those settlements. In the Control Group 88 per cent
of the population (including the children and the elderly people) worked since
they might face starvation if they skipped their work for a single day. In the Program Group the participation rate was only 49 per cent implying a better support
system for the children and the elderly people. Similarly 90 per cent children in
the Control Group were engaged in different types of productive work while in
the Program Group only 6 per cent children were workers - a remarkable improvement considering the background of the Program Group population. The
age profile of the workers presented a similar contrast in the Control Group as
nearly 40 per cent of the working population was children while in the Program
Group only two and half per cent of working population were children. Thus the
author found that the proliferation of child labor in the Control Group was associated with its higher degree of urban marginality in contrast with the Program
Group. This differential position of urban marginality between the two populations was also revealed when the author studied other aspects of the people living these two settlements.

Thus in agreement with the earlier trends the profile of child labor population
also showed a larger proportion of them were between 10 to 14 years and more
than 90 per cent children of that age group worked in the Control Group. Nearly
80 per cent of these child laborers were either not-literate or could sign their
names only. Most of these child laborers in the Control Group were wage earners while in the Program Group working children were engaged in the household
businesses and had much better working conditions. This contrasting trend again
emphasized the need for a change in the paradigm of analyzing child labor problem in a Third World urban situation as urban marginality in terms of urban
space had proved to be a crucial factor in the proliferation of child labor.

It hardly needs reiteration that almost all these child laborers were engaged in
the informal sector of economy. The negligible few employed in the formal sector of economy were assigned to jobs which did not need any record-
maintenance and hence remained invisible from the ambit of formal accounting
and auditing. Most of these child laborers were either rag-pickers (scrap-pickers)
or engaged in the occupations where they needed to sell their labor without any
chance of creating surplus like domestic helps, shoe-shiners, *thonga* (paper-
packet) - makers. As high as 23 per cent of these child laborers, all from the
Control Group, were engaged in work of hazardous nature. Their daily income
mostly ranged between Rs. 10/ and Rs. 25/- (20 cents to 50) after a daunting
working schedule of nearly 10 hours a day in most cases. Some of these child
laborers in the Control Group also had to walk long distances to reach their
workplaces. Thus the occupational scenario of these child laborers, particularly
from the Control Group, was quite similar to the other such child labor situations
in other Third World cities. But here again one found a qualitative difference in
the Program Group where the working children were better treated by their parents and the employers. In fact most of these child laborers in the Program

Group were engaged in their domestic production units under the caring eyes of their parents.

The author also found that most of these children, particularly from the Control Group, worked in with very little or no facilities regarding hazard prevention, self-protection mechanisms, first aid and toilet in their workplaces. The lack of these facilities particularly that of hazard prevention and self-protection had caused frequent accidents and these working children had to bear the brunt of it. These children often had to face harsh behavior both from their fellow adult workers and employers which included physical assaults. Once again it reflected a usual child labor situation in different parts of the Third World as the working children in the Control Group had to face most of these harrowing experiences regarding accidents and harsh behaviors from the employers as well as the fellow adult workers.

On the question of contribution that these children had to make to their family budget to make their family members survive, the author found that the majority of them had to contribute more than 50 per cent of their earnings to their families meaning their families were dependent on their earnings. However, there was a sizable section of them contributed less than 50 per cent of their earnings to their families which might indicate that the proliferation and perpetuation of child labor in a particular population could not always be attributed to the families need to supplement their meager budgets. The author found that more than 71 per cent of the families of these child laborers were substantially dependent on their earnings while nearly 29 per cent of those families were not dependent on the income of their children. It must also be mentioned here that most of these child laborers, in spite of facing poor working conditions, had not left their jobs during their working life. When they left their job they did so due to low pay or accidents or simply got fired for some trivial reasons. Thus in a traditional society like India one should not analyze the relationship between the workers and their employers in the light of the Western concepts of impersonal relationship in the workplaces based on rendering services in return to wages. The author, during this fieldwork, found that in some workplaces the children as well as the adult workers worked under appalling working conditions with very little wages but due to a sense of attachment with the employers they continued working in those conditions and never contemplated leaving their jobs. It was also found during this fieldwork that sometimes the children were compelled to work with low wages and in abysmal working conditions due to various reasons like a sense of security or gratitude from the employers who were the fellow community members or to repay loans that their parents took from the employers or to learn some skilled jobs.

The author resorted to various qualitative methods to understand various aspects of the life of child laborers and their family members. Foremost among them was the study of the attitudes of parents toward their children which showed marked differences between the two groups as parents in the Control Group were less sensitive to the needs of the children compared to their Program Group counterparts. The nature of leisure time activities of the children were also different as the author found that the younger generation in the Control Group spent most of their leisure time outside their households but in the Program Group they tended to spend more within their houses during leisure time. When asked about the cause of spending more time outside their houses, the working children in the Control Group cited the squalid nature of their houses as the reason of their tendencies to spend more time outside their settlements. But in the Program Group the remarkable improvements of living condition as well as the presence of televisions in many houses ensured the young generation to spend more time within their houses.

As a part of the qualitative dimension of this study, the author also tried to observe the world of perception of the working children and their parents on the cause of this problem. It was found that most of these working children attributed the reason for their working to the financial constraints of their parents. Many child laborers, however, thought that they needed a break from the boring study schedule in the school and wanted to do something else. Thus the choice of working was more favorable for them than their study. Most of the parents of these child laborers rationalized the act of sending them for work both in terms of the financial constraints and the futility of formal education coupled with the dire need to learn a skilled job for the safer future of their children.

Thus the author argued that the question of child labor in a Third World city like Kolkata became inextricably bound with various other issues like the vulnerability in terms of urban space or more precisely 'housing poverty' (termed here as the urban marginalization), occupational marginalization, family's apathy to send their children to school, and a tradition of apprenticeship in the area all played big roles in the creation and proliferation of child labor in the Third World cities. There is no denial of the fact that the phenomenon of child labor was one of the main causes of poverty as it created a huge number of unskilled and semi-skilled laborers in the population who could only be absorbed in the ill-paid informal economy. Thus it created a vicious circle of poverty, vulnerability and marginalization. This dimension has not always been adequately stressed by various researchers working on the problem of child labor.

The effect of globalization on the creation of child labor in the Third World cities could also be seen in the present study though a direct correlation between the two might not be readily apparent. Globalization – the flagship of the neoliberal economy – facilitated the international capital and transnational corporations to switch investments across the world. With the growing effect of globalization we see various changes in the Third World countries like the widening gap between the rich and the poor and the rural and the urban, gradual withdrawal of state as a guarantor of more equitable social relations among its citizens, growing unemployment in the Third World, reduced policy options for the Third World countries leading to the reduction in allocations to key social services like food, education, shelter for poor, health etc., privatized key sectors, liberalizing trade, expanding exports and allowing FDI in strategic sectors in these countries.

One major effect of globalization was the proliferation of informal sector particularly in the Third World cities where millions of marginalized people took refuge in the low-paid, strenuous informal works as the job opportunities in the formal sector of economy in these cities did not grow in the same speed in which the rural people lost their livelihoods in the Third World countries. With the spread of globalization and its attendant neo-liberal philosophy the cities were reinvented as the new destinations of capital and as a result huge migrations toward the cities were witnessed particularly during the last two decades. This unprecedented level of migration from the rural areas to the urban centers in the Third World countries was triggered by an exponential increase in unemployment in the villages. The cities became the center of attraction for the new investments and villages were neglected with little or no investments to create new jobs in the rural areas of these countries. Governments also became busy in developing the cities as the international investors were more interested in investing in the urban areas of the Third World. With this huge influx of people from the rural areas, the World cities witnessed an intense struggle over the urban space. On the one hand, the authorities in these cities were busy in implementing city development and city beautification programs to attract new investments. On the other hand, millions of migrants were desperate to create their living spaces within the city for their survival. As a result of this intense struggle over the urban space, the houses of these vulnerable and marginalized people often got demolished by the civic authorities to implement the city development/beautification programs. During this fieldwork, the author found two such settlements of the Control Group population which were demolished by the authority to implement city development programs. These marginalized people lived in those settlements with a constant threat of eviction and the findings from this field suggest that these people released their children for work at a very early age. The author has argued that with the growing influence of globalization and increasing pressure on the authorities to undertake more city development and/or beautification programs in the Third World cities we will see growing proportion of marginalized people who would become vulnerable to these pressures. The uncertain future of these people will compel them to release their children for work. Thus we would see more child laborers as an indirect fall-out of growing influence of globalization in the Third World cities.

The author showed in this book how the confusions regarding the proper definition of child and labor have actually allowed a deferring of the emergence of a proper identification of child labor throughout the world leading to the worldwide misunderstandings on the actual magnitude of the problem. While failure to have any culturally relative definition actually resulted in the dominance of Western concepts and West-mediated ideas on child labor, the author found that "impairment of health and development of children" and "denial of the right to education and opportunity to reach full physical and psychological development" as the most generic characterization of the problem in the Third World. The debates over the usage of the term "child work" instead of "child labor" have also run deep among the researchers on this problem as the first one is considered less value-laden by some than the "child labor". But using the term "child work" as a substitute of "child labor" might fuel new controversies as some observers envisage. One area of diagreement was the fact that "child work" might include activities bordering vagrancy. But during this work, the author found that there was a very little scope of blurring the boundary between the vagrancy and the work in the life of a child in a marginalized population as all the child laborers were consciously engaged in work by their parents. The author also did not find any sense of remorse among parent or the employers as they put the children to work. On the contrary, they did not consider any wrong in taking services from the children as it became embedded in the cultural matrix of these people. The findings from this fieldwork had actually challenged the notion held by many Western observers of independent choice, implying that the children are free to decide whether they want to work or not.

This debate has further brought us to the central issue of how one should analyze the problem of child labor in a traditional society like India. The readers are already familiar with the argument of the author that the phenomenon of child labor in Kolkata should be analyzed in association with the familial background in a traditional society like India. The author observed from this fieldwork that all the child laborers were attached with their families and the families of the child laborers decided how much time the child should allocate to play, study, work or other household chores. The perception of the parents on their children was another important issue responsible for child labor. During this fieldwork, the author found that the parents in the Control Group did not regard their children as a potential resource and they thought that learning a skill from childhood would make their children skilled workers, which was seen as more beneficial for both children and parents rather than sending them to school. This trend was further abetted by the demand for child labor particularly in the area of where the Control Group lived as many occupations and businesses in those areas favored the induction of child labor as it was cheap, easily available and much easier to deploy. Almost all these occupations were from the informal sector of economy where there is greater room engaging child labor as these economic activities function without a strict vigil from the law enforcing agencies. But the author found that the widespread presence of informal economy in the area of the Program Group could not bring children from the wealthier neighborhood in the area to work. This brings us again in front of the need for a new for a paradigm shift in the way of analyzing child labor in the Third World. Thus the author found that in the Program Group the parents considered their children as a potential resource and they tried to lay the foundations for a better for their students by sending their children to school. It was also found that despite poverty an overwhelming proportion of the parents in the Program Group were not prepared to release their children for work at an early age. Thus one should consider the role of the other factors like urban marginalization due to the absence of security of tenure the key determinant for the creation and perpetuation of child labor in the Third World cities. This does not mean that poverty and occupational marginality are no longer the determining factors in the problem of child labor in the Third World cities. As the author found in this field poverty always affects the overall child labor situation in a Third World country. There were fewer child laborers in the Program Group as the inhabitants of this group were more prosperous. An additional argument might be found from the fact that we do not find the similar kind exploitative situation in the developed world as these countries are considerably more affluent than the Third World countries..

Findings from this fieldwork also suggest that child labor was one of the major survival strategies for the poor and marginalized people in the Third World cities to combat urban marginality - a phenomenon seen here as the inability of the market economy or state policies to provide adequate shelter and urban services to an increasing proportion of city dwellers, including the majority of the regularly employed salaried workers, as well as practically all people earning their livelihood in the so-called 'informal' sector of the economy. As already indicated the phenomenon of urban marginalization could not be equated with poverty it was found during this study that urban marginality induced various forms of vulnerability in the life of the marginalized people and the foremost form of vulnerability was poverty. It was also found in this study that in many cases, particularly in the Control Group population, when the processes of marginalization went below a certain threshold, i.e. when the families slipped below a certain level of survival, they sent their children to work. On the other hand, as observed in the Program Group, when a group of people were provided with some kind of security of tenure of their settlements the level of marginalization declined, and so did the incidence of child labor in that group of population.

Thus the author argued that it would be inadequate to postulate that the phenomenon of child labor in Third World thrives only due to abject poverty. But there is no denial of fact that poverty can be a big trigger of child labor. However, there are other factors responsible for the proliferation and perpetuation of child labor, particularly those associated with the globalization and its attendant marginalization of population in the Third World cities. As observed in this study the local authorities had to undertake city development as well as beautification programs in the city to make it more attractive to the investors. The cities in the Third World became the new destinations of footloose investments in the globalized market which rendered a huge proportion of urban population homeless and more marginalized. These marginalized populations, like the Control Group in this study, became the primary breeding ground of child labor as the parents in these marginalized populations tend to release their children for work. Thus globalization played a big role in the proliferation of child laborers. In addition, it was also found that the cultural and social norms also played vital roles in this proliferation. Hence the author favors more such long-term anthropological researches to reach culturally-relative conceptions on child labor i.e. how different cultures view the phenomenon of child labor. More such understandings on the structural inequalities as well as the political and economic circumstances which lead to the phenomenon of child labor in the "Third World" societies would only help to develop a Third World centric understanding of this problem which would an effective tool to combat with this global predicament.

Furthermore, a paradigm shift in the understanding of child labor will help researchers to understand the role of history, politics, social structures, and the economy, as well as race, class, and gender constructions in the growth and proliferation of child labor in the Third World.

1 Nine NCLPs started in areas of high concentration of child labor are:
  a.   Match, fireworks, and explosive industry in Sivakasi in Tamil Nadu.
  b.   Precious stone polishing industry in Jaipur in Rajasthan.
  c.   Glass and bangles in industry in Ferozabad in UP.
  d.   Brassware industry in Moradabad in UP.
  e.   Handmade carpet industry in Mirzapur, Varanasi, and Bhadoi in UP.
  f.   Lock-making industry in Aligarh in UP.
  g.   Tile industry in Jagampet in Andhra Pradesh.
  h.   Slate industry in Markapur in Andhra Pradesh.
  i.   Slate industry in Mandsaur in Madhya Pradesh.
    Subsequently NCLP were launched in Sambalpur, Thane, and Gharwa.

2 According to the 1998-99 annual report of Department of Education (provisional data) drop-out rate in the class I – V in India is 39.58 per cent (49.92 per cent in West Bengal) of them 38.23 per cent are boys (46.17 per cent in West Bengal) and 41.58 per cent are girls (54.15 per cent in West Bengal).

3 In case the child laborer was engaged in the family enterprise where no payment of wage was done, the daily income calculation was done from the estimation of the market price of the amount of production the child could give to the family enterprise and this estimation was done with the help of the head of that enterprise.

BIBLIOGRAPHY

Aggarwal, M.
1995   "International Trade, Labor Standards, and Labor Market Conditions:
        An Evaluation of the Linkages". USITC, *Office of Economics Working
        Paper No.* 95-06-C (June)
Ahmed, F.
1999   *Labor in Informal Sector.* Delhi: Mainak Publications
Appadurai, A.
1990   Disjunction and Difference in the Global Cultural Economy. In M. Fea-
        therstone (ed.) *Global Culture: Nationalism, Globalisation and Mod-
        ernity.* pp. 295-310. Newbury Park, CA: Sage Publications.
Asad, T. (ed.)
1973   *Anthropology and the Colonial Encounter.* Humanities Press: Atlantic
        Highlands, NJ.
Bachman, S. L.
2000   "The Political Economy of Child Labour and its Impacts on Interna-
        tional Business. *Business Economics*, July.
Bagchi, A. K.
1999   Globalisation, Liberalisation and Vulnerability: India and Third World.
        In *Economic and Political Weekly* (Special Articles) Nov 6.

Bagchi, S. S. and A. Das
2004   'On the Question of Urban Poverty in a Third World Context';
        *Journal of the Department of Anthropology; University of Cal-
        cutta*, Vol. 8-9, Issue 1-2.
Bagchi, S. S.
2009   *Expanding Horizons of Human Rights.* New Delhi: Atlantic Publishers.
Bailey, F.G.
1963   'Closed Social Stratification in India,' *European Journal of Sociology*
        4: 107-24.
Baland, J. M. and J. A. Robinson
2000   Is Child Labour Inefficient? *Journal of Political Economy.* 108 (4).
Basu, K.
2003   Marginalization in a Globalizing World: Some Plausible Scenarios and
        Suggestions for Measurement, In C. Edmonds (ed). *Reducing Poverty
        in Asia.* Edward Elgar: Cheltenham, UK.
Basu, K. and P. H. Van
1999   'The Economics of Child labour'. *American Economic Review.* Vol. 88
        (3). p 412-27. June.
Basu, K. and Z. Tzannatos
2003   The Global Child Labor Problem: What do we know and what can we,
        No. do? *World Economic Review*, Vol. 17, No. 2.
Becker, H. and Geer, B.
1960   "Participant Observation: The Analysis of Qualitative Field Data." In
        Adams, R. N., and Preiss, J. (eds.). Human Organization Research:
        Field Relations and Techniques. Homewood, IL: The Dorsey Press.

Benedict, R.
1955   "Continuities and Discontinuities in Cultural Conditioning-1938." In *Childhood in Contemporary Cultures.* Margaret Mead and Martha Wolfenstein, eds. Chicago: University of Chicago Press.

Bissell, S.
2004   "Incentives to Education and Child Labour Elimination". In G. K. Lieten, R. Srivastava and S. Thorat (Eds). *Small Hands in South Asia: Child Labour in Perspective.* Manohar: New Delhi.

Bose, N. K.
1968   *Calcutta, 1964: A Social Survey.* Calcutta: Lalvani Publishing House.
1973   'Calcutta: A premature Metropolis', In K. Davis (ed.). *Cities: Their Origin, Growth and Human Impact.* Pp. 251-62. San Francisco: W. H. Freeman.

Bourgois, P
1995   *In Search of Respect: Selling Crack in El Barrio.* New York: Cambridge University Press.

Boyden, J. E. and P. Holden
1991   *Children in the Cities.* London: Zed Books.

Brown, M., J. Christiansen and P. Philips
1992   'The Decline of Child labour in the U.S. Fruit and Vegetable Canning Industry: Law or Economics?' *Business History Review.* Vol. 66 (4): p 723-70.

Butcher, K. F and A. Case
1994   The Effect of Sibling Sex Composition on Women's Education and Earnings. [Journal Article] *The Quarterly Journal of Economics.* Vol. 109 (3). p 531-63.

Case, A. and A. Deaton
1999   School Inputs and Educational Outcomes in South Africa, *The Quarterly Journal of Economics.* Vol. 114 (3). p 1047-84.

Castells, M.
1977   *The Urban Question: A Marxist Approach.* Translated by Alan Sheridan. London: Edward Arnold (orignal publication in French, 1972).
1983   *The City and the Grassroots: A Cross-cultural Theory of Urban Social Movements.* Berkeley CA: University of California Press.
1993   European Cities, the Informational Society, the Global Economy. In L. Deben, W. Helinemeijer, and D. Van der Vaart. (eds.).*Understanding Amsterdam: Essays on Economic Vitality, City Life and Urban Form.* Madrid: Sistena, DI.

Castells, M. and J. H. Mollenkopf.
1991   *Dual City: Restructuring New York (The City in the tewenty-first century).* New York: Russell Sage Foundation.

Census of India
1961   *Housing and Establishment Tables,* table E-1, New Delhi: RGI, Government of India.

1971   *Housing Tables,* table IV-B, New Delhi: RGI, Government of India.

1981a   *Housing Tables,* table H-I, New Delhi: RGI, Government of India.

1981b   *Household Tables,* table HH-l, New Delhi: RGI, Government of India.

Childe, V. G.

1950   The Urban Revolution. *Town Planning Review* 23: 3-17.

Cornia, G. A., R. Volly and F. Stewart (Eds)

1988   *Adjustment with a Human Face: Ten Countries Case Studies.* Vol. II. Oxford: Oxford University Press.

de la Luz Silva, M.

1981   "Urban Poverty and Child Work: Elements for the Analysis of Child Work in Chile", in Garry Rodgers and Guy Standing (eds.) *Child Work, Poverty and Underdevelopment.* Geneva: ILO.

Department of Education, MHRD

1999   *Annual Report 1998 – 1999.* New Delhi: Department of Education, MHRD, Government of India.

Dev. M. S.

1996   'Social Security for Indian Workers: Performance and Issues,' *Indian Journal of Labour Economics,* Vol. 39, No. 4.

Dutt, A. and A. Mukhopadyay

1993   "Slum dwellers' daily movement pattern in a Calcutta slum". *GeoJournal,* vol. 29, No. 2, pp. 181–186.

Escobar, A.

1988   "Power and Visibility: The Invention and Management of Development in the Third World. *Cultural Anthropology.* 3(4): 428-443.

FEANTSA.

1999   "Strategies to combat homelessness in Western and Eastern Europe: trends and traditions in statistics and public policy", report prepared for UNCHS (Habitat), Nairobi. Brussels: FEANTSA

Fox, R. G.

1967   'Family, Caste and Commerce in a North Indian Town'. *Economic Development and Cultural Change.* 15:3, 297-314.

1972   Rational and Romance in Urban Anthropology. In *Urban Anthropology.* 1: 205-33.

1977   *Urban Anthropology: Cities in Their Cultural Settings.* New Jersey. Prentice-Hall.

Fyfe, A.

1989   *Child Labour.* Cambridge: Polity Press.

Garg, A. and J. Morduch

1998   Sibling Rivalry and the Gender Gap: Evidence from Child Health Outcomes in Ghana. *Journal of Population Economics.* Vol. 11 (4). p 471-93. December.

Geertz, C.

1960   *The Religion of Java.* Chicago: University of Chicago Press.

70   Bibliography

1968a   *Agricultural Involution: The Process of Ecological Change in Indone-*
         sia. Berkeley, CA: University of California.
1973   *The Interpretation of Cultures*. New York: Basic Books,
1988   *Works and Lives: The Anthropologist as Autho*r. Stanford: Stanford
         University Press.
Ghosh, D. N.
1999   Globalisation and National Politics. In *Economic and Political Weekly*.
         Sept. 25.
Goddard, V. and B. White
1982   "Child Workers in Capitalist Development: An Introductory Note
         and Bibliography", in *Development and Change*, Vol. 13, No. 4,
         October.
Government of India, National Commission on Urbanisation
1988   *Report*. Vol. II. New Delhi: Government of India.
1991   *Instruction to enumerators for filling up the household schedule and*
         individual slip. Office of the Registrar General and Census Commis-
         sioner for India, Ministry of Home Affairs, New Delhi: Government of
         India.
Government of India, Ministry of Health
1988   *Health Information, India*, New Delhi: Government of India.
Grootaert, C. and R. Kanbur
1995   "Child Labour: An Economic Perspective". *International Labour Re-
         view*. 134: 187-201.
Gugler. J.
1991   'Overurbanization Revisited', In Gilbert, A. and J. Gugler, 1991. *Cities,
         Poverty, and Development: Urbanization in the Third World*. Oxford:
         Oxford University Press.
Hannerz, U.
1969   *Soulside: Inquiries into Ghetto Culture and Community*. Chicago: Uni-
         versity of Chicago Press.
1980   *Exploring the City: Inquiries towards an Urban Anthropology*. Colum-
         bia University Press: New York.
1990   Cosmopolitans and Locals in World Cultures. In M. Featherstone (ed).
         Global Culture: Nationalism, Globalisation, Modernity. Newbury Park,
         CA: Sage Publications.
1992   *Cultural Complexity: Studies in the Social Organization of Meaning*.
         New York: Columbia University Press.
Henderson, J. and M. Castells (eds).
1987   *Global Restructuring and Territorial Developmen*t, London: Sage Pub-
         lications.
Hendrick, H.
1997   *Children, Childhood and English Society, 1880-1990*. Cambridge:
         Cambridge University Press.
ILO (International Labour Organization)

1998   *Child Labour: Targeting the Intolerable.* Geneva: International Labour Organization.
2001   *World Employment Report 2001.* Geneva: International Labour Organization.
Institute of Applied Manpower Research
1995   *Status and Problems of Leather Workers and their Future Growth Perspective: A Study Based on Survey on Leather Workers in Unorganized Sector in the Districts of Agra.* New Delhi: Institute of Applied Manpower Research.
Jafarey, S. and S. Lahiri
2002   "Will Trade Sanctions Reduce Child Labor? The Role of Credit Markets". *Journal of Development Economics.* Vol. 68.
James, A. and A. Prout
1997   *Constructing and Reconstructing Childhood: Contemporary Issues in the Sociological Study of Childhood.* London: Falmer Press.
James, A., C. Jenks and A. Prout
1998   *Theorizing Childhood.* Cambridge: Cambridge University Press.
Jensen, R. T.
1999   "Patterns, Causes and Consequences of Child labour in Pakistan," mimeo, *John F. Kennedy School of Government, Harvard University,* June.
2000   "Agricultural Volatility and Investments in Children," *American Economic Review,* May, 90(2): p. 399-404.
Karunanidhi, G.
1995   *A Study on the Beedi Workers of North Arcot District.* New Delhi: ICSSR.
Kearney, M.
1986   "From Invisible Hand to Visible Feet: Anthropological Studies of Migration and Development." *Annual Review of Anthropology* 15:331-361.
Kemper, R. V.
1975   Directory of Urban Anthropologists. *Urban Anthropology* 4: 73-106.
1991a Urban Anthropology In The 1990's: The State of Its Practice. *Urban Anthropology and Studies of Cultural Systems and World Economic Development* 20: 211-223.
1991b Trends in Urban Anthropology Research: An Analysis of the Journal Urban Anthropology, 1972-91. *Urban Anthropology and Studies of Cultural Systems and World Economic Development* 20: 373-84.
1993   Urban Anthropology: A Guide To U.S. and Canadian Dissertations. *Urban Anthropology and Studies of Cultural Systems and World Economic Development* 22: 1-229.
Kemper, R. V. and J. Rollwagen

72   Bibliography

1995   Urban anthropology. In Ember, M. and D. Levinson, (eds.). *Encyclope-
          dia of Cultural Anthropology*. Lakeville: American Reference Publish-
          ing.
Kumar, B. and G. Biswas
1992   *A Study of Problems of Working Children in Lock-making
          Industry, Aligarh, (U.P.)*, Allahabad. New Delhi: Manohar.
1992   *A Study of Problems of Working Children in Brassware Industry
          of Moradabad (U.P.)*. Allahabad. New Delhi: Manohar.
Kundu, A.
1993   *In the Name of the Poor: Access to Basic Amenities*. New Delhi: Sage
          Publications.
Kumar, N.
1992   *Friends, Brothers and Informants: Fieldwork Memoirs of Banaras*.
          Berkeley, CA: University of California Press.
Leeds, A. and R. Sanjek
1994   *Cities, Classes, and the Social Order*. Ithaca, New York: Cornell Uni-
          versity Press.
Levinson, D., A. Richard, S. Ashraf and S. Barge
1996   Is Child Labor Really Necessary in India's Carpet Industry? *Labor
          Market Papers*, 15.
Lewis, O.
1961   *The Children of Sanchez: Autobiography of a Mexican Family*. New
          York: Vintage.
1966a   "The Culture of Poverty," *The Scientific American* 215 (4): 19-25.
1966b   *La Vida: A Puerto Rican Family in the Culture of Poverty*. New York:
          Vintage.
1970   *Anthropological Essays*. New York: Random House.
Lewis, O., R. M. Lewis and M. Mead
1975   *Five Families: Mexican Case Studies in the Culture of Poverty*. New
          York: Basic Books.
Liebow, E.
1967   *Tally's Corner: A Study of Negro Street Corner Men*. Boston: Rowman
          and Littlefield.
Lieten, G. K. and B. White
2001   *Child Labour Policy Options*. Amsterdam: Aksant.
Magubane, B.
2000   *African Sociology: Towards a Critical Perspective: Selected Essays of
          Bernard Makhosezwe Magubane*. Trenton, NJ: Africa World Press.
Maitra, M. S.
1991   Shelter: Slums and Squatter Settlements. In Government of West Ben-
          gal Publication. *Calcutta's Urban Future: Agonies from its Past and
          Prospects for the Future*. Calcutta: Government of West Bengal.
Margo, R A. and F. T. Aldrich

1996 'Compulsory Schooling Legislation and School Attendance in Turn-of-The Century America: A 'Natural Experiment' Approach.' *Economics Letters*. Vol. 53 (1). p 103-10. October.

Maskus, K. E.
1997 Should Core Labor Standards be Imposed through International Trade-Policy? *Policy Research Working Paper Series* 1817. The World Bank.

Mead, M. and M. Wolfenstien (eds.)
1955 *Childhood in Contemporary Cultures.* Chicago: University of Chicago Press.

Menon, S.
1979 "Sivakasi: The 'Little Japan' of India," *The Times of India*, October 7.

Mintz, S. W.
1977 "The So-Called World System: Local and Initiative Response." In *Dialectical Anthropology* 2(4), 253-270.

Moehling, C. M.
1999 State Child Labor Laws and the Decline of Child Labor. *Explorations in Economic History*, 36.

Morduch, J.
2000 "Sibling Rivalry in Africa," *American Economic Review*, May, 90(2), p. 405-409.

Morrice, A.
1981 "The Exploitation of Children in the Informal Sector: Proposals for Research"; in Garry Rodgers and Guy Standing (eds.) *Child Work, Poverty and Underdevelopment.* Geneva: ILO.

Mukherjee, S.N.
1970 'Class, Caste and Politics in Calcutta, 1815-38', In E. Leach and S.N. Mukherjee (eds.). *Elites in South Asia.* Pp.201-22. Cambridge: Cambridge University Press.

National Institute of Urban Affairs
1988 *Who the Poor Are? What they Do? Where they Live?* New Delhi: National Institute of Urban Affairs.

National Sample Survey Organisation (NSSO)
1987a *Table with Notes on Particulars of Dwelling Units*, NSS, 38th Round, Department of Statistics, Ministry of Planning and Programme Implementation, New Delhi: NSSO.

1987b *Tables with Notes on Particulars of Dwelling Units,* Thirty-eighth Round (Jan-Dec 1983), Number 339. New Delhi: NSSO.

1989 *Morbidity and Utilisation of Medical Services*, NSS, 42nd Round, Department of Statistics, Ministry of Planning and Programme Implementation, New Delhi: NSSO.

1990 'A Profile of Households and Population by Economic Class and Social Group and Availability of Drinking Water, Electricity and Disinfection of Dwelling', 42nd Round, *Sarvekshana*, 13(4), Government of India, New Delhi: NSSO.

1997a   Slums in India, NSS 49th Round, Department of Statistics, Ministry of
         Planning and Programme Implementation, New Delhi: NSSO.
1997b   *Dwellings in India*, NSS 50th Round, Department of Statistics, Ministry
         of Planning and Programme Implementation, New Delhi: NSSO.
1998a   Housing Conditions in India, NSS 49th Round, Department of Statistics,
         Ministry of Planning and Programme Implementation, New Delhi:
         NSSO.
1998b   *The Aged in India: A Socio-Economic Profile*, Department of Statistics,
         Ministry of Planning and Programme Implementation, New Delhi:
         NSSO.
1998c   'Attending an Educational Institution in India: It's Level, Nature and
         Cost,' *NSS 52nd Round, July 1995-June 1996, Report No.439*; Depart-
         ment of Statistics, Government of India, New Delhi: NSSO.
1998d   1997 — NSSO 53rd Round as reported in Selected *Educational Statis-
         tics; 1998-99*, Department. of Education, MHRD Table 13, New Delhi:
         NSSO.
2001   *Employment and Unemployment Situation in India – 1999 – 2000, Part
         I, NSS 55th Round (July 1999 – June 2000), Report No. 458*; Ministry of
         Statistics and Programme Implementation, New Delhi: NSSO.
NCAER
1999a   'Micro Impacts of Macroeconomic and Adjustment Policies' (MIMAP)
         – *India*, October. Volume 1, Issue 1
1999b   *India Human Development Report of the Nineties.* New Delhi: NCAER.
Nieuwenhuys, O.
1996   "The Paradox of Child Labor and Anthropology." *Annual
         Review of Anthropology.* 25: 237-251.
Palley, J. I.
2002   "The Child Labor Problem and the Need for International Labor *Stan-
         dard. Journal of Economic Issues,* 35: 601-605.
PREALC
1978   *Sector Informal: Functionamiento y Politicas.* Santiago: PREALC.
1991   *Empleo y equidad: eldesafio de los 90.* Santiago: PREALC.
Ranjan, P.
2001   Credit Constraints and the Phenomenon of Child Labor. *Journal of De-
         velopment Economics.* Elsevier, Vol. 64(1).
Redfield, R.
1947   'The Folk Society'. *American Journal of Sociology* 52: 293-308.
1955   *Peasant Society and Culture: An Anthropological Approach to Civiliza-
         tion.* Chicago: University of Chicago Press.
Registrar General of India
1981   *Census of India*; Provisional Population Totals: Workers and Non-
         workers, Paper 3, Series 1. New Delhi: RGI.
1996   *Census of India 1991. Part IV, Social and Cultural Table.* New Delhi:
RGI.

1997a   *Census of India 1991; Age, Sex and Educational Level, Table C-2.* New Delhi: RGI.

1999a   *Compendium of India's Fertility and Mortality Indicators 1971 to 1997.* Based on Sample Registration System. New Delhi: RGI.

1999b   *Ageing Population of India: An Analysis of the 1991 Census Data.* New Delhi: RGI.

2001   *Provisional Population Totals, Paper 1,* 2001 Statement 19. New Delhi: RGI.

Rodman, M.

1992   'Empowering Place: Multilocality and Multivocality'. *American Anthropologist.* 94: 640-56.

Rodrik, D.

1997   *Has Globalisation Gone Too Far?* Washington, DC: Institute for International Economics

Ruark, J. K.

2000   "Seeing Children and Hearing Them, Too." In *The Chronicle of Higher Education.* November 17, 2000: A22-A24.

Said, E. W.

1978   *Orientalism.* New York: Pantheon.

Sargent, C. and N. Scheper-Hughes, (eds.)

1998   Small Wars: The Cultural Politics of Childhood. Berkeley: University of California Press.

Schildkrout, E.

1981   "The Employment of Children in Kano (Nigeria)", in Garry Rodgers and Guy Standing (eds.) *Child Work, Poverty and Underdevelopment.* Geneva: ILO.

Sharma, A. N., R. Sharma and N. Raj

2000   *The Impact of Social Labelling on Child Labour in India's Carpet Industry.* ILO/IPEC Working Paper. New Delhi: Institute for Human Development

Shelburne, R. C.

2001   An Explanation of the International Variation in Prevalence of Child Labour. *World Economy,* 24: 359-378.

Singh, M., V. D. Kaura and S. A. Khan

1980   *Working Children in Bombay – A Study.* New Delhi: National Institute of Public Cooperation and Child Development.

Sjoberg, G.

1960   *The Preindustrial City: Past and Present.* Cambridge: The Free Press.

1964.   'Further Comments on the Preindustrial Cities,' *Sociological Quarterly* 5 (Spring): 144-47.

Southall, A. (ed.)

1961   *Social Change in Modern Africa.* London: Oxford University Press.

1973   *Urban Anthropology: Cross-Cultural Studies of Urbanization.* Oxford: Oxford University Press.

1999   *The City in Time and Space.* Cambridge: Cambridge University Press.

Spar, D. L.

1998   The Spotlight and Bottom Line", *Foreign Affairs*, 77: 7-12.

Stephens, S. (ed.)

1995   *Children and the Politics of Culture.* New Jersey: Princeton University Press.

Suttles, G. D.

1968   *The Social Order of the Slum: Ethnicity and Territory in the Inner City,* Chicago: The University of Chicago Press.

Swaminathan, M.

1995   "Aspects of Urban Poverty in Bombay", *Environment and Urbanization*, Vol. 7, No. 1.

1999   'Economic Growth and the Persistence of Child labour: Evidence from an Indian City.' *World Development.* Vol. 26 (8). p 1513-28.

Szanton Blanc, C. (ed.)

1994   *Urban Children in Distress: Global Predicaments and Innovative Strategies.* Florence: UNICEF.

UNCHS (Habitat)

1991   *Assessment of Experience with the Project Approach to Shelter Delivery for the Poor.* HS/241/91 E, Nairobi: UNCHS.

1993   *National Trends in Housing-Production Practices. Volume 1: India.* HS/310/93 E, Nairobi: UNCHS.

1994   *National Experiences with Shelter Delivery for the Poorest Groups.* HS/308/93, Nairobi: UNCHS.

1995   *Global Report on Human Settlements 1995.* Nairobi: UNCHS.

1996a   *The Human Settlements Conditions of the World's Urban Poor.* HS/391/96 E, Nairobi: UNCHS.

1996b   *An Urbanising World: Global Report on Human Settlements*, Nairobi: UNCHS.

1997   *Shelter for All: The Potential of Housing Policy in the Implementation of the Habitat Agenda.* HS/488/97 E, Nairobi: UNCHS.

2000   *Strategies to Combat Homelessness.* HS/599/00 E, Nairobi: UNCHS.

2001a   *Cities in a Globalizing World: Global Report on Human Settlements 2001.* London: UNCHS.

2001b   *The State of the World's Cities Report 2001*, Nairobi: UNCHS.

2001c   *The Istanbul Declaration and The Habitat Agenda.* HS/411/97/E, Nairobi: UNCHS.

UNCHS (Habitat) and the International Labour Office (ILO).

1995   *Shelter Provision and Employment Generation.* HS/339/94, Nairobi and Geneva: UNCHS and ILO.

UNCTAD

(several years) *World Investment Report,* Washington: UNCTAD.

UNDP (United Nations Development Programme)
1990   *Human Development Report, 1990*. New York: UNDP.
1995   *Human Development Report 1995*. Oxford: UNDP.
1998a   *Human Development Report, 1998*. New York: UNDP.
1998b   *Overcoming Human Poverty: UNDP Poverty Report 1998*. New York: UNDP.
UNICEF (United Nations Children's Fund).
2002   *The State of the World's Children 2002*. New York: UNICEF.
United Nations
1958   Multilingual Demographic Dictionary, *Population Studies No. 29*, New York: United Nations.
1990   *World Urbanization Prospects 1990*. New York: United Nations.
1995   *Programme of Action of the World Summit for Social Development*. New York: United Nations.
1996a   *The Right to Adequate Housing*. Prepared by Rajindar Sachar, Special Rapporteur of the Sub-Committee on Prevention of Discrimination and Protection of Minorities, Centre for Human Rights, Geneva: United Nations.
1996b   *World Urbanization Prospects: The 1996 Revision*. New York: United Nations.
1998   *Principles and recommendation for population and housing censuses*. Statistical Papers, Series M No.67/Rev.1. Sales No. E.98.XVII. 8, New York: United Nations.
United Nations, Department of Economic and Social Information and Policy Analysis.
1997   *World Economic and Social Survey 1997*. New York: United Nations.
Venkatarayatta, K. N.
1957   *Bangalore: A Socio-Ecological Study*. Bombay: Popular Prakashan.
White, A. G.
1975   *Urban Anthropology: A Selected Bibliography*. Monticello: Council of Planning Librarians.
Whyte, W. F.
1943   *Street Corner Society*. Chicago: University of Chicago Press.
World Bank
1988   "Access to Basic Infrastructure by the Urban Poor", *EDI Policy Paper No. 28*, Washington, D.C: World Bank.
1990   *World Development Report 1990*. Washington, D.C: World Bank.
1992a   *World Development Report 1992*. Washington, D.C: World Bank.
1992b   *Global Economic Prospects and the Developing Countries*. Washington, D. C.: World Bank.
1995   *Social Impact of Adjustment Operations*. Washington D.C: World Bank.
1997   *World Development Indicators*. Washington (D.C.) : World Bank.
1999a   *World Development Report 1998/99*. Washington, D.C: World Bank.

1999b *Global Economic Prospects and the Developing Countries 2000.* Washington D.C: World Bank.

2000a *Poverty Online Debate.* http://www.worldbank.org/devforum/ forum_globalisation.html (Accessed in June 19, 2001.): World Bank.

2000b *World Development Report 2000/2001.* Washington (D.C.): World Bank.

2001 *Global Development Finance.* New York: World Bank.

(several years) *World Development Report.* New York: World Bank.

World Health Organization

1992a *Our Planet, Our Health.* Report of the Commission on Health and Environment. Geneva: WHO.

Zelizer, V. A.

1985 *Pricing the Priceless Child: The Changing Social Value of Children.* New York: The Free Press.

APPENDICES

APPENDIX I

State-wise Distribution of Working Children according to 1971, 1981, 1991 and 2001 Census in the age group 5-14 years

S. No.	Name of the State/UT	1971	1981	1991	2001****
1	Andhra Pradesh	1627492	1951312	1661940	1363339
2	Assam *	239349	**	327598	351416
3	Arunanchal Pradesh	17925	17950	12395	18482
4	Bihar	1059359	1101764	942245	1117500
5	Delhi	17120	25717	27351	41899
6	Goa			4656	4138
7	Gujarat	518061	616913	523585	485530
8	Haryana	137826	194189	109691	253491
9	Himachal Pradesh	71384	99624	56438	107774
10	Jammu & Kashmir	70489	258437	**	175630
11	Karnataka	808719	1131530	976247	822615
12	Kerala	111801	92854	34800	26156
13	Madhya Pradesh	1112319	1698597	1352563	1065259
14	Maharashtra	988357	1557756	1068427	764075
15	Chhattisgarh				364572
16	Manipur	16380	20217	16493	28836
17	Meghalaya	30440	44916	34633	53940
18	Jharkhand				407200
19	Uttaranchal				70183
20	Nagaland	13726	16235	16467	45874
21	Orissa	492477	702293	452394	377594
22	Punjab	232774	216939	142868	177268
23	Rajasthan	587389	819605	774199	1262570
24	Sikkim	15661	8561	5598	16457
25	Tamil Nadu	713305	975055	578889	418801
26	Tripura	17490	24204	16478	21756
27	Uttar Pradesh	1326726	1434675	1410086	1927997
28	West Bengal	511443	605263	711691	857087
29	Andaman & Nicobar	572	1309	1265	1960
30	Chandigarh	1086	1986	1870	3779
31	Dadra & Nagar Haveli	3102	3615	4416	4274
32	Daman and Diu	7391	9378	941	729
33	Lakshadweep	97	56	34	27
34	Mizoram ***		6314	16411	26265
35	Pondicherry	3725	3606	2680	1904
	Total	10753985	13640870	11285349	12666377

Note: * 1971 Census figures of Assam include figures of Mizoram.

** Census could not be conducted.

*** Census figures 1971 in respect of Mizoram included under Assam.

**** includes marginal workers also.

APPENDIX II

Hazardous industries, occupations, activities and agents most frequently cited in national legislation on child labor (Source: ILO 1998: 107-108)

Prohibited industries and occupations	No. of countries
Mining, quarries, underground work	101
Maritime work (trimmers and stokers)	57
Machinery in motion (operating, cleaning, repairs, etc.)	57
Weights and loads	40
Construction/and or demolition	37
Circular saws and other dangerous machinery	35
Lead/zinc metallurgy	34
Transportation, operating vehicles	33
Entertainment	32
Alcohol production and/or sale	29
Cranes/hoists/lifting machinery	23
Crystal and/or glass manufacture	22
Welding and smelting of metals	20
Agriculture (specified tasks only)	14
Abattoirs and meat rendering	14
Underwater work	13
Street trades	12
Production of pornographic material	10
Tanneries	12
Textile industry (specified tasks)	5
Metal and wood handicraft (different tasks inc. carpentry, slate-pencil production, precious stone work)	7
Forestry	6
Brick manufacture	5
Explosives (manufacturing and handling)	50
Fumes, dust, gas and other noxious substances	35
Radioactive substances or ionizing radiation	29
Chemicals, general provisions for exposure to	26
Pathogenic agents, exposure to (hospital work, city cleaning, work related to sewers, handling of corpses)	18
Electricity	15
Paints, solvents, shellac, varnish, glue or enamel	19
Asbestos	8
Benzene	5

INDEX